Tears   le

Learnin

"You have collected all my tears
in your bottle."
Psalm 56:8

By
William H. Griffith, D.Min.

Author of
More Than a Parting Prayer
Lessons in Care Giving for the Dying

XULON
PRESS

Copyright © 2010
by William H. Griffith, D.Min.

Tears in a Bottle
by William H. Griffith, D.Min.

Printed in the United States of America

ISBN 9781609573461

All rights reserved solely by the author. The author guarantees all contents are original and do not infringe upon the legal rights of any other person or work. No part of this book may be reproduced in any form without the permission of the author. The views expressed in this book are not necessarily those of the publisher.

Unless otherwise indicated, Bible quotations are taken from the New Revised Version of the Bible, Copyright © 1989, Division of Christian Education of the National Council of the Churches of Christ in the United States of America.

www.xulonpress.com

Endorsements

All persons involved in care giving, from the clergy to the lay member of a pastoral care team, will find William Griffith's latest book, *Tears in a Bottle,* a valuable resource in their ministry to and with the bereaved. This book has the feel of a conversation with the author as he weaves the reader through reflection on biblical stories of grief, his own experiences as both a pastor and hospice chaplain, and his reflective questions for the reader. The reader will feel the pull and tug of Griffith's words and questions helping him or her to confront personal experiences in grief, connect them with biblical reflection, and the practice of care giving. Griffith reminds us of the importance of the ministry work in bereavement, calling us to give focus, time and attention to all of the grief's in life and death. *Tears in a Bottle* is an excellent book for individual growth and will even be richer when shared and discussed with a group.

Rev. Daniel Cash, D.Min.
Senior Pastor, First Baptist
Church, Columbus, IN

Tears in a Bottle points all who are grieving to the lives of familiar biblical personalities to learn from their experiences. Through personal reflection exercises, William Griffith helps us reflect on our own grief as we journey through this book. He also sensitively takes your hand and helps you walk through the grieving process. With encouragement, support and guidance, he smoothes the ragged, empty, painful journey of healing. He calms the restless heart by providing hope and understanding.

David P. Gallagher, D.Min.
Program Director,
Green Lake Conference Center,
Green Lake, Wisconsin,
Author: *Healing Takes Time*

Having worked with Bill Griffith for several years in Hospice, I have seen him up close working with patients and staff. He has a heart for God and a love for people, especially the bereaved. This book shares the principles he has used to bring healing to his patients and clients. *Tears in a Bottle* takes a little known text and brings it to life. The writer takes several Biblical stories and relates them to his own life experiences with the grieving. My heart was touched by these real-life illustrations. This book will be valuable for individuals experiencing loss, and for groups gathered to support each other in grief. I will enthusiastically recommend it to my patients and clients. How comforting it is to realize we are never alone, and God cares about every tear we shed.

Thomas A. Long, M.Div.
Hospice Chaplain and
Bereavement Counselor,
Columbus, IN

Grief is a universal experience, yet it's not instinctive to grieve well. Nor does our culture support the grief process. So, most of us just want it over with. But there's a better way. With hope as the foundation, William Griffith challenges the reader to grow in the ability to grieve. The significance of this growth may not be as obvious as it is profound: Those who grieve well, live well. Dr. Griffith provides a wide spectrum of stories from the Bible and contemporary life that will encourage the reader to trust God for hope and healing. Those who have experienced loss will readily find a common bond with the stories in this book.

Rev. Dr. Myrlene Hamilton Hess, Author of *On the Road to Emmaus: A Travel Guide for Those Who Grieve* Pastor of Morning Star Presbyterian Church, Bayville NJ

This book presents in accessible language the good news of hope and healing in the face of loss and grief. William Griffith deftly integrates personal story and biblical narrative, psychological and theological insight, and clinical wisdom stemming from many years of counseling and chaplaincy practice. He thus helps us to better understand the dynamics of growth through suffering. Most importantly, he invites us to reflect deeply on our own experience of loss and grief and offers practical guidelines not only for self care but also for caring well for those around us facing loss.

Daniel S. Schipani, Dr. Psy., Ph.D., Professor of Pastoral Care & Counseling, Associated Mennonite Biblical Seminary and author of: ***The Way of Wisdom in Pastoral Counseling***

This book is dedicated to the memory of:

Orie "Buck" Griffith 4/07/12 – 11/28/07
My Father, whose religious disciplines and work ethic helped shape my life.

Virgil Taylor 5/12/17 – 7/05/06
My woodworking mentor and friend, who taught me and encouraged me on my creative journey.

Dennick Skeels 10/20/52 – 5/02/08
My Friend, whose baptism, wedding, and memorial services will always remind me of the importance of commitment and dedication to family and friends.

Acknowledgements

This is not a book I wanted to write because it forced me to journey again in the valley of the shadow. Yet, it is because of that journey and the experience of God journeying with me, which gently nudged me to write.

I am also thankful for friends who read the manuscript and offered words of encouragement to pursue all avenues to see that it was published.

For those who read the manuscript and wrote endorsements I am deeply indebted. My respect for their insights and words of affirmation confirmed my own conviction that it is in the sharing of stories that we are able to get in touch with our own story.

My creative wife Lois put down her quilting needle and rug hook long enough to sharpen her pencil and critique the entire manuscript. I value her insights greatly.

I also appreciate my daughter Karen Kreider, who found time in the midst of her busy life as wife, professional woman, and mother of nine month old Gavin, to do a final editing before publication.

And finally, I have been personally blessed again and again, by God's faithfulness in collecting my tears and journeying with me.

Contents

Preface

One of the major themes of the Bible is evident in the reoccurring stories of people experiencing grief. Individuals, families, and nations are confronted with experiences of loss, and the struggle to redefine their hope. Writers document the variety of their experiences in order to help future generations discover the lessons they have learned.

Genesis is the book of "beginnings", and in the first two chapters we learn that God was pleased with what was created. *"And God saw that it was good."* No grief stories in those first two chapters.

Chapter three is the beginning of grief. The result of Adam and Eve's disobedience is described in verses 7 & 8, *"Their eyes were opened and they knew that they were naked...and they hid themselves from the presence of God."*

They lost their innocence and their privileged relationship with God. Then in verse 23 their grief continues, *"God sent him forth from the garden of Eden."* They not only lost their homeland and all that was familiar to them, but the good life they valued would one day end in death. From that point on the biblical story documents how persons experienced their many losses.

Three chapters later in 6:6-7, after multiple stories of grief and loss there are those astonishing words *"And the Lord was sorry that he had made humankind on the earth, and it grieved him to his heart."* At the very outset of biblical story God grieves.

So what does God do? Divine hope is redefined. God started over with a man named Noah. The Rainbow became God's sign of redefined hope and promise. It was a time of new beginnings, but grief and sorrow would continue as a major part of the biblical story.

The biblical storyline is that persons are always losing what they value, and losing what is valued is what grief is all about. The good news is what God does for them at such a time. Throughout the telling of the stories of grief God reassures those who are grieving that their grief does not go unnoticed by their God. In Psalm 56:8 David says, *"You keep track of all my sorrows. You have collected all my tears in your bottle; you have recorded each one in your book."* [1] David experienced confidence and comfort knowing that his sorrow, sadness and tears did not go unnoticed by God. Our confidence and encouragement to redefine our hope when we experience grief and sorrow comes also from knowing God notices our tears as well.

The tears that God collects are the expected normal expression of biblical sorrow. *"There's a time to weep... and a time to mourn..."* (Ecclesiastics 3:4) The Bible includes an entire book of Lamentations that is about weeping and sorrow. Those who expressed their grief were reminded in a variety of ways that God not only collected their tears but shared their grief. *"Surely he hath borne our grief's and carried our sorrows."* (Isaiah 53:4 KJV). From Eden to Calvary, to the new Heaven and new Earth of the book of Revelation, grief and hope are two sides of the same biblical coin. The beginning of grief is in Genesis, and it continues until the biblical story of God collecting tears ends in Revelation, where we read *"God will wipe away every tear from their eyes."* (Revelation 21:4)

Out of the hundreds of biblical stories of grief, the focus of this book will be to examine selected stories as examples of the grief process where persons shared their tears, worked through their grief and redefined their hope. By examining their journeys of grief, and remembering God was collecting their tears and recording their sorrow, we reaffirm that God also does that for us. Their stories provide insights into our own experiences of grief, and the importance of our effort to redefine hope. "*Many of the basic principles of grief therapy as spelled out in modern psychological and clinical research are already present in scripture.*" [2]

One of those basic principles is how important support is for the one who grieves. Even Jesus, when he experienced his anticipatory grief in the Garden of Gethsemane, took his disciples along with him. "*And he took with him Peter and the two sons of Zebedee, and began to be sorrowful and very heavy. Then saith he unto them, 'My soul is exceeding sorrowful, even unto death...'*" (Matthew 26:37-38 KJV).

In the biblical narratives which follow, it is God who comes along side and shares the journey providing the comfort necessary to not only endure the sorrow, but to get through it. What we learn from these stories may best be described in 2 Corinthians 1:3-4 when Paul states, *"Praise be to the God and Father of our Lord Jesus Christ, the Father of compassion and the God of all comfort, who comforts us in all our troubles, so that we can comfort those in any trouble with the comfort we ourselves have received from God."* (KJV)

The following stories are from both the experiences of persons in the Bible as well as those from the present day. As you read them, there will be questions for reflection inserted at various places so that you will be able to reflect on your own story and discover how well you have learned to grieve.

Introduction:

The Importance of Hope

Hope is a word that has been devalued and often needs to be redefined.

It is devalued because it is so familiar and often over used. It is not uncommon for words to fall into a lesser state of importance. Love and faith also qualify for this classification. These words have been key players in the formation and the interpretation of major theologies, psychological theories, as well as many self-help books. They are of course the well recognized threesome which summarizes the biblical chapter on love. *"And now faith, hope, and love abide, these three; and the greatest of these is love."* (1 Corinthians 13:13).

All three words become part of our vocabulary very early in life, if not in knowing how to define the words, we have at least known the exercise of each. Children are no strangers to hope. Parents quickly make a promise to a child that if they will do (or not do) something then the parent will respond with an offer of something that will please the child. "If you put all of your toys away, then mommy will buy you an ice cream cone." The child is given a reason to hope. The parent, in an effort to accomplish a task and teach a discipline, is also providing an experience that teaches the child the importance of hope. Then when the child accomplishes the task he or she continually reminds the parent of what was promised. The child's reminder is an effort to bring about the fulfillment of what his or her hope has been.

We began to learn the lesson as a child that hope is most valued when it is measurable. The anticipation of what was hoped for had a powerful controlling influence over how we acted. There was a future moment that shaped the present waiting. Then when that which was hoped for had arrived, we gave ourselves permission to return to behaving in our more normal way.

This training exercise in hope is an attitudinal formation that provides us with the necessary inner strength to enable us to live each day. Hope is a powerful magnetic force that pulls us into our future. It defines what makes life meaningful.

Without this hope, persons experience despair and depression and conclude there is little reason to live. In Greek mythology, the story about Pandora illustrates this. "Pandora had been given a jar and instructed by Zeus to keep it closed, but she had also been given the gift of curiosity, and ultimately opened it. When she did, all of the evils of mankind escaped from the jar, although Pandora was quick enough to close it again and keep one value inside, and that was Hope." [1]

When Pandora realized the awful thing she had done, she sat down and began to cry. "Pandora heard a small sweet voice ask, "Pandora, can you please release me?"

"Why should I? Didn't you see who they were?"

"Of course I did, they are my sisters. But I can assure you I am not like them." Pandora who felt all was lost sadly opened the box. A beautiful sprite with gossamer wings flew shimmering into the sunlight. Round and round her body the creature flew lighting only when a sore was encountered. As the creature touched the hurt — it was gone. When Pandora had been healed completely the creature flew to heal Epimetheus. Pandora sat back against the box and thought. Hope, she was certain that was the creature's name, continued her healing.

In time the sprite flew back and rested exhausted on Pandora's shoulder. Pandora watched as the creature drifted painlessly into her flesh and took up residence in her heart. She knew she had been given the gift that, even though it could not erase the pain she had brought to the world, could make that pain easier. She smiled a soft smile for knowing there is hope, and hope is sometimes enough. [2]

Unexpected troubling life circumstances often rob a person of the ability of seeing any meaning in the future. Until such a person identifies and hopes for some future expectation, they remain imprisoned. They have been taken hostage by their circumstances.

One of the major life experiences that tend to take a person hostage is the experience of losing something or someone who has been valued. We know this experience by the more familiar generic word "grief". But when we use the word "grief" we are likely to think only of death, and that limits our learning and under-standing of the larger life lesson con-cerning loss of any kind.

- A person loses a job;
- A child loses a toy;
- A teenager's family moves her away from her closest friend;
- A community loses its major employer;
- A married couple gets a divorce;
- A doctor diagnosis a terminal illness;
- A baby is stillborn;
- A teenager doesn't make the team;
- The dog dies.

The list is endless. Each of us could add more personal illustrations of those life events where we have lost something of value and have not known where to turn or what to do. It is into such a moment that hope must be redefined. Something must be identified that gives us reason to believe that life is still worth living. Loss shatters hope. Hopelessness is learned early on in life from the nursery rhyme.

Humpty dumpty sat on a wall
Humpty dumpty had a great fall.
All the kings horses, and all the kings men
Couldn't put Humpty together again [3]

The childhood nursery rhyme is sad because there is no hope, and when we conclude our life circumstances are hopeless we reach that level of sadness. Our feeling is that we will never put life together again.

It is at such a time that we often need someone outside ourselves to help us process our way back. Counseling, simply put, is hearing the state of hopelessness in another and enabling them to redefine hope as an effort to believing their future is important.

That kind of outside help may be in the form of a person or sometimes it is in the form of reading material that offers a glimpse into a slice of life with which a person may identify. It is my hope that this book will provide some helpful biblical examples of how others, as part of their faith journey, have had to redefine hope, and through their stories we will be encouraged to discover the value of such possibilities.

Redefining hope is not merely an option for one who is grieving; it is a necessity if one wants to survive and move on. Hope needs to be redefined because grief is the result of a hope destroyed. Any redefinition of an experience means accepting the experience, and that's easier said than done. It's much easier to look back and to know that we HAVE moved beyond a prior grief, than it is to confront grief and deal with the overwhelming emotions of it in the present. However, if we have some biblical models of those we respect, whose tears have been collected in God's bottle, we will surely find encouragement and strength when confronted with our own grief work.

When the Apostle Paul wrote, *"... you may not grieve as others do who have no hope"* (1 Thessalonians 4:13), he was attempting to get the attention of the Christian who was having a difficult time dealing with the emotional loss that comes when a loved one dies. He was reminding them of the two basic teachings that are at the very heart of the Christian Faith; the power of the Resurrection and the coming of Christ. He encourages the followers of Christ to put their grief in this larger context by redefining their hope in light of that teaching.

In a broader more general way, he is applying the principle that the basis of a person's spirituality ought to be the source from which a person draws his strength and courage to come to terms with death and grief. Whatever defines a person's spirituality during life must contain that teaching which enables a person to deal with those unwanted circumstances that relate to grief.

Ira Byock, M.D. in his book *Dying Well* writes, *"...the realms of spirit and soul is, of course, influenced by one's culture, religious tradition, family life, philosophical perspective, and life experiences, but it is inherently intimate and deeply personal."* [4]

As a hospice chaplain, I have discovered that any person experiencing grief needs to ask how those spiritual values which have guided them in living will now support them in redefining hope for their future.

In my book *More Than a Parting Prayer,* I tell the story about a woman who lived life as an Agnostic. [5] Her story illustrates how we process those spiritual values at the end of life and how those values either support us on our journey or they give us reason to question those values. Her assumption was that because she had a fear of dying, everyone faced dying in the same way. She longed for a peace that her values never shaped within her, and hearing that others had values which gave them such peace caused her to want to know more.

The major stories in the Bible are stories about persons dealing with loss and grief, and how they processed their grief and redefined their hope. When we examine these stories from the Bible about persons who were grieving we must ask what it was from their culture, religion, family life and experience that provided them with the ability to redefine hope.

Ashley Prend, in her book *Transcending Loss,* suggests that those who see opportunity in crisis, who look for open rather than closed doors, have certain qualities and characteristics in common. She offers the acronym called SOAR: *Spirituality, Outreach, Attitude, and Reinvestment* as the pathways through which persons move in order to reach the ultimate healing stage that she calls Transcendence.

She defines Transcendence as *"...rising above your immediate circumstances, achieving a new perspective, and in so doing, discovering possibilities for a future."* [6]

Given the universal nature of grief and the importance of each person processing their grief, we will examine biblical stories to see how persons were able to redefine hope and how they moved through their grief to Transcendence.

So many biblical stories are about people who were confronted with circumstances beyond their control when they lost something they dearly valued. The writers paint pictures of disappointment and despair and tell of how they faced and overcame their unwanted circumstances. By examining their journeys, we are able to identify what they went through and gain insights and confidence about the process we must go through if we are serious about our desire to redefine our hope.

Through their stories, we see them as human as we are. They were not exempt through some divine intervention from confronting sorrow and loss, but they were comforted by the divine presence that shared their journeys.

Joseph's grief resulted from his brother's decisions. Naomi's grief began with a loss of homeland. Job's grief is a biblical tale of 'Murphy's law', if anything can go wrong it will. The two Emmaus disciples grieved the loss of their historic hope. As each one grieved, God collected their tears as he does ours.

Along with these biblical stories I will share the grief journeys of friends I met as a hospice chaplain. Through your reading and reflection of your own story, you will be looking back and remembering, but you will also be affirming those values which will better prepare you for your next loss. Through biblical reflection and personal story you will gain a new appreciation for God's faithfulness in also collecting your tears.

1

Joseph
The Loss of More than a Colorful Coat

Genesis 37-50

Joseph's story, the longest narrative in all of scripture, is about redefining hope, culminating in his being able to look back on all the losses and discern how God was with him through it all.

When Joseph was sold by his own brothers to a caravan of traders headed to Egypt, he must have had the normal feelings of loss of everything he once valued. Added to that hurt and loss was the knowledge that it was caused by the actions of his own brothers. His future was bleak compared to his life as a privileged son of Jacob. But that's getting ahead of our story.

Joseph, as a seventeen year old teenager, enjoyed the favoritism of his father Jacob and his brothers were jealous. Joseph alienated his relationships with his brothers by telling them his dreams, and the dreams elevated his status over them, and how they would eventually have to recognize and accept it.

Jacob's family dynamics were very dysfunctional. Any family that promotes favoritism of one child over the other creates animosity and jealousy among the siblings. Joseph's brothers experienced the loss of that expression of their father Jacob's love which they saw Joseph receiving. The coat of many colors was the symbol of their loss as much as it was Joseph's position of favor. The brothers saw an opportunity to rid themselves of the one who caused them so much grief and they took it.

When Joseph went out to the fields where his brothers were sent to work, he showed up wearing his favorite coat of many colors and his brothers plotted to kill him. What a shock it must have been to Joseph to have had his coat taken from him and then be thrown into the pit. As the plot unfolded, he must have feared for his life believing they would kill him. At seventeen years of age he no doubt experienced a great deal of fear and uncertainty of not being in control of his circumstances. He was too young to die. Life wasn't fair.

Personal Reflection
Do you have a memory from your teenage years when you felt "Life isn't fair?" From your adult years?

Joseph was experiencing spiritual pain. *"Spiritual pain is actually the result of the breaking of two illusions: first, I am in control of my own being; and second, I am in control of the relationships around me."* [1]

Personal Reflection
What is your memory of experiencing "spiritual pain"? How recent?

Joseph was not in control of his life, and his dream of being in control over his brothers appeared to be more a nightmare than a divine dream.

While in the pit, his brothers were eating and discussing his fate. They came for him to take him out of the pit, not to kill him, but to sell him to some Midianite traders who were passing by. What mixed feelings Joseph must have had. He was not going to lose his life, but he was going to lose his family, his home and his place of privilege.

Given the multiple losses he experienced we have to wonder at the outset of this narrative just how he will ever be able to find his way through his grief. Lynette J. Hoy, a grief counselor on her web site addresses the issue of how persons are able to get through their grief and move on. She writes in answer to the oft asked question,

"**What do you need to do to get to the point of living with the loss in a healthy way?** *These four steps can be helpful for most types of losses.*

1. You need to change your relationship with whatever you lost.
2. The next step is to develop your own self and your life to encompass and reflect the changes that occurred because of your loss.
3. The third step is discovering and taking on new ways of existing and functioning without whatever it was that you lost.
4. The fourth step is to discover new directions for the emotional investments that you once had in the lost object, situation or person." [2]

When we examine the Joseph narrative in light of these four steps, we are able to recognize that his actions and attitudes mirror what these steps suggest.

His very first step had to change his relationship with his brothers. He must have been angry with them and fearful of what they might do. In this early phase of Joseph's grief it appears he was able to cope because the worst that could have happened to him didn't. His brothers could have killed him, but they didn't. Sometimes that is exactly what we experience when we've lost all that we once valued. The circumstances still feel out of our control, but some event happens that enables us to balance it with what the alternative might have been, and we see a glimmer of hope. Our anger and shock is not so overwhelming because we live to see the light of another day.

This is what we hear victims of natural disasters saying when they have lost their home and all their possessions, but have not lost their lives. They realign their priorities in light of the loss and see something for which they can hope.

We do not know to what degree Joseph suffered and experienced spiritual pain. Suffering is different than spiritual pain in that suffering is how we interpret our loss or our inability to make any sense of it.

Joseph's suffering would have been defined by his knowing his life had been spared and he was not going to die. His spiritual pain was that he was going to be separated from his father and family and lose everything he had been taught to value. His relationship with his brothers would never be the same, and I do not sense that his earlier dream of superiority over his brothers gave him any reason to accept their actions. If anything, they proved they were more superior to him than he ever realized. It was the dream, and no doubt the coat of many colors, that created the jealousy and hostility the brothers were acting out. The relationship he once shared would have to change, and at this point in his life it may have been that he might never have a relationship with them again.

Personal Reflection
What loss have you experienced where you realigned your priorities and even reevaluated your relationships?

The next step for Joseph was that he had to develop his own self and know that his losses would have a major impact on redefining him.

Joseph didn't know where he was going or what he would do. The circumstances of his life would continue to be directed by other person's choices. The traders would get paid by someone and he would become someone's slave. He didn't have the power to change those circumstances, but he knew he had to cope with them, and understand how they would change him. He could at least make the most out of whatever circumstances he had to face, because he was alive.

Personal Reflection
What loss have you experienced that you feel most defines who you have become?

Persons experiencing suffering must draw upon a source outside themselves for the needed courage and strength to carry on. It is this

source that enables a person to interpret their suffering while at the same
time look for ways to redefine their
hope for the future.

Joseph's Hebrew religious culture and tradition not only provided
instruction regarding a God who
provided strength and courage for
persons who were suffering; those
teachings were interwoven with his
own genealogy. The stories about his
grandfather Isaac, and great grandfather Abraham, would have been family
stories that were becoming culturally
and traditionally significant. Joseph
would have heard about Abraham's
going out not knowing where he was
going and hearing how God provided.
He would have heard about the miracle birth of his grandfather Isaac and
how his life was blessed by God. He
had some very important role models
who must have provided the resolve
to trust God to provide for him also.
And God did provide.

Joseph became a trusted servant of
Pharaoh and was given great responsibility over Pharaoh's entire house,

and this turn of events is credited to Joseph's God. Joseph's hope was in knowing that his God would provide. It is here that we see Joseph taking step three in moving through his grief. That step is discovering and taking on new ways of existing and functioning without whatever it was that he had lost. He was bought to be a servant and he applied himself in ways that made him a trusted servant. That quality of trust had to have been earned by the way he carried out his expected duties for Pharaoh. For Joseph it was a new way of functioning. He no longer lived in a world of relationships where he was looked upon as being special and where he himself had servants. He became a servant and in this new role he was able to demonstrate a knowledge and work ethic that got the attention of the Pharaoh. Joseph did not allow the losses that once defined him to limit him from seeing the opportunities that helped him redefine his hope.

We know however that the story does not end here. But Joseph, like all of us must endure additional losses. Grief is not so much a journey where we have a beginning and then a destination that signals we are now finished with that journey, as it is a life long process. For Joseph and for us, there are those times when we feel good about having worked through a process of grief, only to be overwhelmed again by another loss. Joseph lost his reputation when he refused the sexual advances of Pharaoh's wife, she lied to get even and he was thrown in prison. Once again he must have gone through the litany of unfairness trying to make sense of why he deserved this fate. Once again he has to deal with his loss of position, power, and reputation because of the actions of another person's untruthfulness, and once again he has to discover the inner resolve to cope with it. He would have to go back and work through his prior steps.

In prison, he established his reputation and a new self image with the other prisoners and they discovered that he had the unique ability to interpret dreams. The Chief Cup Bearer and the Baker shared their dreams, and what he predicted was correct for both of them. The cup bearer's life was spared as he predicted, but the baker's life was taken from him by Pharaoh. Joseph must have hoped that the Chief Cup Bearer would have remembered him when he was freed and put in a good word for him with the powers that be. But he didn't. And so the opportunity for Joseph was lost, and he remained in prison. Joseph, however, was able to redefine his seemingly hopeless plight because of his cultural, religious, and family teachings. He continued to cope because he continued to believe that God would provide. Two years passed and he still remained in prison. The process of moving toward wholeness is not simply defined in weeks or months, but is uniquely individual to a person and their particular loss. Because one person appears to have processed their grief in six months ought never to create the expectation that we, or anyone else, should be able to do the same. Grief is not resolved or worked through in a manner that is predictable. The many variables of personality, relationships, level of emotional investment, and available support will all have a bearing on the length of time it takes for an individual to work through to a healthy self.

One day Joseph's reputation of being an interpreter of dreams was shared with Pharaoh by the Cup Bearer who had been in prison with Joseph. The Cup Bearer gave Pharaoh the account of how the dreams were interpreted by the Hebrew who was also in prison. Pharaoh immediately called for Joseph's release so that he could interpret his troubling dream. Joseph interpreted Pharaoh's dream of the coming famine and was immediately given authority to oversee all of Egypt so that all would survive the coming drought. Here again, Joseph takes on a new way of existing and begins to function again as a faithful servant.

Once again Joseph faced a future that appeared to be a lot brighter than his past. He moves on to step four where he discovers new directions in which he can place his emotional investment. His hope and confidence in his God was once again rewarded. The years of coping and hoping gave him reason to reaffirm his confidence and trust in God. It had been thirteen years since he was thrown into the pit and sold by his brothers as a slave, but he never stopped hoping.

During the next seven years when there was prosperity in the land, and before the seven predicted years of famine Joseph settled down and made Egypt home. He began a new level of investing his emotional energy. He began his family with the birth of two sons, and the names he gave them indicated how he had understood his life in Egypt. *"The first born he called Manasseh, 'For...God has made me forget all my hardship and all my father's house.'"* (Genesis 41:51).

Personal Reflection
What new ways and relationships redefined you after experiencing a major loss?

Joseph was marking the progress of his movement from having had to give up all that he valued, to his acceptance of how life must now be lived. His statement does not mean that he could ever forget all that happened, but he was not allowing the memory of how his brothers betrayed him and sold him to keep him from moving forward. His realization of how far he had come gave him reason to mark the progress with the naming of his first son.

When his second son was born he named him Ephraim, *"For God has made me fruitful in the land of my misfortune."* (Genesis 41:52). He recognized that all of his experiences in the new land had not been positive, but the sum total of what had happened to him deserved to be noted as a blessing from God. His spirituality, based on his family, tradition, and values sustained him and enabled him to hope.

The rest of the story is about Joseph meeting his brothers when they came to Egypt looking for grain during the famine, and how he toyed with them as they depended upon him for their survival. His early dream had come true and they did bow down to him. The difficulty of reunion is evident as the brothers confessed their guilt and wrong doing and asked for forgiveness knowing that their lives might be in danger. Joseph shows them no malice but demonstrates he is not burdened down with the baggage of the past. The faith by which he lived and endured the hardships and the inner strength that enabled him to cope through his many losses now provides him the wisdom to embrace his brothers and to relieve them from their guilt by saying, *"So it was not you who sent me here, but God..."* (Genesis 45:8).

Joseph had made a life for himself in spite of his brothers, and appears to have been surprised at their showing up and needing his help. His early dream had been put on hold for many years, and its fulfillment had to have been more satisfying than just filling their sacks of grain. Being reunited with his brothers and family was surely more than he ever dreamed.

Personal Reflection
Do you have an experience of holding on to hope for many years? Are you experiencing that now?

Looking back through the stories of his trials in captivity as well as his blessings Joseph was able to see the bigger picture of how God had provided for all of them. In each instance he had to redefine hope based on his confidence in a God who would provide for him every bit as much as God provided for Abraham. His belief system was the foundation which determined his attitude toward life.

It is no different for us. All of us can discover much about our faith by looking back and seeing how overwhelming circumstances were eventually used by God for our own good. It is our belief system, which is the foundation for our attitude. Knowing of those past experiences and how our beliefs shape our attitude will help to prepare us for redefining hope when grief overwhelms us in the future.

Joseph, in the midst of his own loss chose not to have a 'pity party' but instead to reach out to others in prison and get beyond his own circumstances and reinvesting himself in the needs of others. Outreach enables a grieving person to see life from a larger perspective, and encourages reinvestment of the emotional capital that was lost.

I remember a loss I experienced as a Pastor. I was in the interview process with a search committee and was told a decision would be made on a certain day. The day came and the call came and I was told they had chosen to present another candidate to the church. I was emotionally at a loss. I hung up the telephone, sat down in a chair and didn't know what to do next. My mind was trying to process the loss, trying to make sense out of it and in the midst of my confusion and loss the telephone rang. A church member was calling to tell me her husband had just died after three long years of battling a disease. She asked me if I could come and be with her. I went. And what I learned in going was that in reaching out to another in need and getting outside my own loss and reinvesting my energy in another, I was able to view life as being much bigger than the world of my emotions.

That's what Joseph's life illustrates for us as he continually has to keep his eye on a picture bigger than his own emotional loss. His life illustrates how the exercise of redefining hope is an ongoing process of moving through the work of grief toward acceptance and Transcendence.

Joseph's story is filled with wonderful lessons and eternal truths that are applicable to our own lives. But woven through all the varied and diverse experiences is the way he had to deal with grief. That is one of the major lessons we must not overlook.

Personal Reflection
Identify how you took steps to reinvest your emotional energy after a loss.

Chapter 2

Tears from the Soul

In my role as a hospice chaplain, I frequently have a patient who is identified in the medical chart as having dementia. Alzheimer's is one of the many diseases that cause dementia. A person afflicted with dementia often communicates incomplete thoughts and sentences in a manner that indicates they know what they are talking about but the hearer isn't able to connect the dots of their thought process. There is some discussion among health care professionals as to the value of providing spiritual care for such a person. The debate is between those who believe a person has a soul residing within the physical body of the person with dementia, and those who do not.

I know as a hospice chaplain the challenge of not allowing the cognitive impairment of the individual to keep me from seeing the soul within the physical body. When a dementia patient provides no reasonable, logical feedback to the conversation that is shared, every effort is made to connect with something familiar, especially something that may be religious or spiritual. Sometimes I quote familiar scriptures and pray the Lord's Prayer in hopes that it might connect with their thought process. There have been times when such a connection has been made for a very brief moment, only to be set aside for another subject.

The most positive interaction I have had with a person with dementia, that validates for me the ability to connect to their soul, happened one day while visiting a patient in an extended care facility.

I entered the room and took my normal seat on the edge of her bed, while she sat in her recliner. The patient was an 85 year old widow. We had known each other over the twelve years that I was her pastor, but I had left that church fifteen years before. In my retirement years I returned to the community and became a part time hospice chaplain, and she was one of the patients assigned to me.

In my four previous visits with this patient, who I will call Wanda, she showed no evidence of relating to any of my conversation about our past experiences together as her pastor. My reminder to her of her husband's name and their faithfulness as members of the church did not appear to trigger any signs of connecting to me and the church.

On this particular visit, I sat with her and listened to her disconnected stories, trying to mimic the feelings I saw in her face and tone of voice. She was always content with the stories she told and would appear to anyone watching us from a distance that we were having a great conversation. As she was speaking to me she said that "The Lord will take care of it, he always does." I repeated it back to her saying, "You are so right, the Lord always takes care of us."

She then bowed her head, closed her eyes and began a prayer, "God, you will take care of us..." She continued by naming her husband and asking God to take care of him. Her husband has been deceased for many years. She named others I did not know and asked God to take care of them. She referred to situations unknown to me, but which were very troubling to her and continued to speak to God in a very direct manner. Twice during her prayer she prayed for her pastor and his family, and I could only wonder if my spirit had connected with her spirit and she was praying for me. She did this for over two minutes never opening her eyes or shifting into a conversation with me. Only toward the end did her phrases begin to sound like unconnected communication, but to her it was part of her praying. She came to the end with a long pause, and then simply said "Amen" and she opened her eyes.

I said to her as I continued to hold her hand, "God hears your prayers, and God loves you very much." As she looked at me, a tear came from each eye. She didn't speak, but in that moment I had connected with the soul of one who had been in communion with God, and whose tears were expressions of feelings that could not be put into words.

A few moments of silence passed between us and then she began talking to me in phrases that were again unrelated and had no content that had any meaning for me.

Two tears were shed one from each eye, from a body that housed a brain held prisoner by dementia, but whose soul was alive and well. Two more tears for God to collect. I thought of Romans 8:16 as an affirmation of this experience. "*It is that very Spirit bearing witness with our spirit that we are children of God...*"

Personal Reflection
What experiences have you had relating to a dementia patient? What were your frustrations? What were your joys? What did you learn?

Chapter 3

Naomi's Journal
A Lifetime of Grief

Ruth 1-4

Journaling is a recommended way to help persons relieve stress and sort out the unwanted circumstances that so easily overwhelm the spirit. A hospice web site suggests that *"Journaling will give you a place to express your pain, frustration, fear, loneliness...Journaling also allows you a safe place to ask, and 'Where is God in my experience?' As you write, you uncover God's hand in your life."* [1]

The following is an imaginary journal of Naomi, the mother-in-law of Ruth. In it we see how she uncovered God's hand in her life as she worked through her multiple grief experiences, and how we can apply her lessons to our situation today.

Journal entry One:
I don't want to go.

Today has not been a good day. The weeks of famine have turned into months and we have so little to eat. Elimelech has decided we must leave Bethlehem and find a place to live where there is food. He has heard that the famine has not hit the people of Moab, so he plans on taking us there. It is a difficult decision leaving our home, our family and friends, but with two sons we both know it must be done. I don't want to leave; it's the only home I've ever known. I will miss everyone. I cry but try not to let him see me. I know he's doing what has to be done. I'm also scared knowing that we will be living in a foreign country and not knowing how we will be accepted. I wish we didn't have to go. **N.**

Moving is a loss and may create a great deal of grief, especially when the move is not a personal choice but forced because of circumstances. It is even more difficult when the move is to a place that is foreign; a place where there are no family members; where persons speak a different language and have different culture and food customs. Such an experience is stressful because we are thrown into the arena of change. We do our best to rationalize the changes as being necessary, and we identify in our minds how important those changes will be, but in the depth of our being we are grieving deeply. At that time we 'make the most of it' and 'do the best we can.' We are hopeful that the reason for our change will be validated by the new experiences we have.

Personal Reflection
What loss/grief experiences have you had because you moved? What did you lose?

Throughout my thirty-five years of pastoral ministry I moved to five different churches. Each move was initiated by a search committee looking for a pastor, and the resulting process was a choice my wife and I made together. Each move was different and became more complicated as our three children became part of the equation. Believing that each move was following God's will gave us the assurance that we were in the place God wanted us to be. Knowing that gave us confidence about where we were going, but it didn't lessen the emotional losses we experienced.

When I decided to retire from pastoral ministry the idea of moving presented a different challenge. We owned our own home, and some persons assumed we would just stay in the community. We didn't consider that as an option for a variety of reasons. Since we had never lived near either of our families, we chose to move to Arizona where my wife's sister and brother and family lived. Our three children were no longer living in the home, so the two of us could move anywhere we desired.

The move was good, although it provided new experiences of loss for us. It was the first time we had moved without having a built-in community of support that we had known when we moved to our previous churches. For the first time in our lives we discovered what it was like to go 'shopping' for a church. Our weekly evaluation of our Sunday experience only highlighted our losses. Filling the void of fellowship and friendship was at the top of our 'shopping list'. Finding a church worship service that enabled us to experience worship was not easy. Our comfort in worship was based on years of being the one responsible for creating it, and the loss of that made the choice of another even more difficult. After three months of searching we finally discovered a place of worship, fellowship, and friends, but the process was one that demanded redefinition of our hopes and expectations.

Naomi no doubt was able to accept the change when her husband was able to find food and provide for her and her sons. They settled down and made a new home for themselves, and just about the time she became comfortable accepting the changes of her environment she experienced another tragic loss.

Journal entry Two:
My Husband Died Today

*Today Elimelech died. I am an emotional basket case. I don't know what I'm going to do. My sons are so helpful and are working and they tell me not to worry. They tell me they will take care of everything. They have both been talking about two girls they have met and they are interested in marrying them. I guess that is good, but that means we will never go back home to Bethlehem. I was so hoping we could return home, but if that's what is best for them, then it will be all right for me. They are so good to me. **N.***

Death is the ultimate loss, and I can only imagine Naomi's grief was compounded by the fact that her husband's death did not happen in her homeland where family and friends could support her.

At such a time, we tend to rationalize that if the tragic loss we experienced had only happened under different circumstances it would in some way be more acceptable. Our intellect works overtime trying to create scenarios that would be more acceptable to our emotions. This is the process of grief work where we live between the tension of the past and what was, and the future and what will be. It is our way to redefine hope and will give us something to live for.

Personal Reflection
During an experience of loss/grief did you ever feel like "This is not a good time for this to happen?"

As a hospice chaplain, I have often been with people when some tragic shattering news is shared and a common tearful response is, "This is such a bad time for this to happen."

Depending on how well I know the person, I may respond by saying, "If you had to write this in your Day-Timer calendar, where would you write it?" My effort is to help the person face up to the reality that their painful experience would not be any more pleasant by rescheduling it.

The intellectual exercise, however, may be the needed stop gap measure our psyche needs to briefly buffer the shock of the loss. Being able to imagine some other time and some other place as being better in some way is an effort to be in control of the uncontrollable. The loss of what we have valued is an experience of being confronted with the reality that we are not as much in control of life as we often assume.

The compounded grief of Naomi brings together the prior loss of her homeland with her husband's death and she has every reason to be a 'basket case.' In the midst of such compounded grief, it is important for a person to find some ray of hope so that they will not allow the depression of the spirit to overcome them. Day after day they continue their routine as best they can until something good begins to give them hope that their future will be brighter than their past.

Personal Reflection
When have you experienced multiple losses? What did you hope for?

Our retirement move to the Arizona desert carried with it the hopes and dreams of enjoying the freedom to reinvent ourselves and spend time investing energy in the things that would make us happy. That's when I became a part-time chaplain for a local hospice; played tennis and golf with new friends; and honed my woodworking skills in my woodshop. Just when everything seemed to be the way we intended it to be, we were confronted with unplanned circumstances. My wife's sister was diagnosed with Leukemia and needed a bone marrow transplant, and my wife was the best possible donor match.

Following the transplant, my wife became the primary caregiver for the next two years.

We began to see our retirement move as having a bigger purpose than 'fun in the sun'. Our schedules were adjusted and my wife provided the loving care her sister needed. We adjusted our schedules and redefined our hope in terms of different priorities. What we had to do was not what we would have chosen to do, but we made new choices based on the circumstances that presented themselves. What we gave up doing represented a loss that had to be seen as it related to the larger picture.

Personal Reflection
Have you experienced a time when you had to give up personal goals because a loss/grief made you examine the bigger picture? How did you feel?

Naomi, once she adapted to her new surroundings and began to be comfortable in her new homeland, had to enter the grief process again with the death of her husband. She would once again have to intentionally work at redefining her hope for her future. She would grieve, wrestling with the decision of whether or not to move back to her homeland, knowing her sons had reasons to stay. She must have been lonely.

Journal entry Three:
My boys get married

Mahlon and Chilion came to me today wearing big smiles on their faces. They said they had good news to share with me. I said, "Well, what is it?" Together in chorus they said, "We're going to get married." I hope I didn't appear too shocked. I guess I always knew they would get married, and I had always thought I'd find for each of them a good Jewish girl to make them happy. Good Jewish girls are hard to find here in Moab, so I braced myself for the news when I asked. "And just who are the lucky girls?" Both wanted to speak first, and neither would let the other

73

be first, so I got both stories at once. When they finished I knew the girl's names were Orpah and Ruth, but couldn't remember which was marrying which. I gave them each a hug and told them I was happy for them, but wished they could have married Jewish girls instead. They gave me their typical reply, "Oh Mama," when I questioned their decisions.

I guess I have to accept it; after all it wasn't their decision to come to Moab. **N**.

Often when we are redefining our hope, we reach a plateau of contentment as we accept the unacceptable unwanted circumstances. We process our loss and discover that life does go on and we must get on with living. What becomes the norm is not necessarily what we might have chosen, but we discover that we have been able to make the necessary adjustments.

Before the death of a spouse it is impossible to imagine how life could be lived without that relationship. To compound that grief is to have the death occur far from home without all the familiar support systems which are so necessary. To be a single mother of two sons in a foreign land is not a circumstance anyone would ever schedule. Such circumstances demand that hope once again must be redefined, and having "been there and done that," a person knows it will take a lot of work to do it again. Although each grief encounter is a new experience, there is an accumulated confidence that it can be faced once again.

Such life circumstances teach us that we might not always get the "full loaf" and we have to settle for "half a loaf." Naomi had to be pleased that her sons were moving on in their grief and were able to make such an important decision. They were redefining their hope in the selection of a wife. Their decision must have helped her redefine her hope as well. She had reinvested her emotional energy in her sons, and now two daughters-in-law would need some of that emotion as well.

Journal entry Four:
My boys are dead.

I can't believe this. For ten years we have been a happy family, and although I may have nagged about wanting grandchildren, it's better they had none. Both of my boys are dead. If they had had children then the children would not have a father. I am very angry because God has turned against me. It's unfair! I don't deserve this. First I must move away from my family and come to this 'god-forsaken land' only to have my husband die here. Now my two sons, who were so happy, even with Moabite wives, are both dead. That's not the way it's supposed to be. Children shouldn't die before their parents. When is God going to 'cut me a break?' I can't stay here any longer, I have to go back home to be with my people. I have nothing to live for...especially here. **N**.

Multiple losses create additional anger about the fairness or unfairness of the circumstances we experience. People of faith often believe they deserve better. Their attitude reflects an assumption that because they have faithfully practiced their religious rituals, God ought to check the ledger and "cut them a little slack." Religious people may feel this unfairness but they may never verbalize it because to verbalize it might anger God. It might also display a lack of faith and give others reason to question their faith commitment.

Personal Reflection
Has any loss/grief made you feel "God isn't fair?" Were you able to express that? Why: Why not?

Some reach the point of giving up on God because redefining hope is a hard lonely experience. Some persons seem to face hard times over and over, while others breeze through life with very few hard experiences. It's hard enough the first time, but when you talk yourself into having to do it the second time you live on the edge of acceptance. The third time is not a charm when it comes to losing what you value most in life; you're no longer on the edge, you're in the pits.

Personal Reflection
What was your most devastating loss/grief that made you feel you would never be happy again? What happened to enable you to redefine your hope?

The year my wife's sister died, my mother also died, and then eleven months later, our sister-in-law also died, leaving her husband and two teenage children who lived near us. Our multiple grief experiences made us very familiar with the litanies of unfairness that haunted us in the depths of our being.

During that time, I was not only working as a hospice chaplain with dying patients and families but also I was writing the manuscript for my book, *More Than a Parting Prayer: Lessons in Care giving for the Dying.* I was both blessed and frustrated as I knew in my mind all the intellectual information that was necessary to process my grief, but getting the information from my mind to my heart was a different story. The wisdom of the old saying is true; the longest journey in the world is the sixteen inches between the mind and the heart.

Having faith at such a time is often difficult. Remember the story of the man who was walking along a trail in a mountainous park and he slipped and fell over the edge? He clung to the root of a tree which grew out of the mountain side. In the darkness he cried out for help. "Is there anyone up there?" Someone heard him and realizing there was ledge just inches below the man's feet said, "Let go. You'll be fine." The man hanging by the root replied, "Is there anyone else up there?".

At such a time, when faith is so difficult, it is understandable that a person wants to go back to the familiar and return to the environment where there are relationships and memories that are supportive. We want to be with the people with whom we share a common history. The decision to return is full of hope, and it is more than just hoping for a change of scenery, it is particular scenery which is hoped for. It is a return to one's roots, to the place where one was nourished by tradition and religious teachings that gave meaning to life. To return is to be hopeful that such meaning would also return.

Naomi decided to go home.

Journal entry Five:
Telling Orpah and Ruth

I told them tonight that I was returning to my homeland and they surprised me with their response. They both said they were going to go with me. When I assured them I could make the journey alone, they said they didn't mean they would travel back with me so I would have someone to share the journey; they wanted to go back and live with me there. I was startled by their expressions of love for me and the following morning we started out together.

The next morning we hadn't traveled far when I felt this was all wrong. They should not go with me. They did not belong back in Bethlehem. They were Moabite girls who would not fit into our culture because our people had some very strict rules. When we stopped for a rest, I told them that it wasn't right for them to think they needed to return to my homeland with me. I gave them all kind of reasons why they had no obligation to do so, and encouraged them to go home and marry a good Moabite boy and raise a family. I told them I was just bad luck, and they deserved better. I blessed them for what they had done for me in showing me their love and devotion. I kissed them and turned to go my way. They began crying loudly and begging me not to leave them. They both smothered me with kisses, and Orpah said her goodbyes, let go of me and turned around and headed home. Ruth wouldn't let go of me. I tried to shame her saying she should go be with her sister and go back to her people and worship their gods, but she would hear none of it.

She made a promise and vowed to not leave me but to return with me. She even said she was willing to make my God her God. That was really startling since I wasn't even sure I wanted my God to be my God.

She was so determined I knew I could not change her mind, so I gave up trying.

I have no idea how this is going to work out. **N.**

Whenever a person experiences multiple losses it usually shakes the foundation of whatever faith values they have lived by. There comes a time when a person feels that they need a change of scenery. It's not that by nature of the mere change their luck will change, but it is a hopeful decision that starting over somewhere else might be best. There are times when a person may choose to go somewhere which will guarantee anonymity; as if not being known will guarantee that the grief from the known losses will not follow. There are other times when a person desires to get back to what is familiar; to the neighborhood and environment which once was so safe. It is more than a trip down memory lane that is being hoped for, it is a return to those symbols of support that will hopefully still provide the needed encouragement to "keep on keeping on."

Family, tradition, culture, and the faith values that shaped her were at the heart of Naomi's decision to return to Bethlehem. She must have felt like she had nothing more to lose, so why not go back to where everybody knows your name. Given that her emotional tank was on empty, she didn't have sufficient energy to keep Ruth from returning with her. She must have been encouraged by the way Ruth insisted. She must have begun to feel that there was one person on her side after all. Knowing she did not have to return alone no doubt carried a mixed set of emotions. Ruth's love was a great support, and because of it she would do all she could to help Ruth find acceptance among her people. Naomi knew what it was like to be a foreigner in a strange land, and she would intentionally see to it that Ruth was welcomed.

Personal Reflection
What experience of love and support have you experienced during your loss/grief that surprised and blessed you?

That is a decision many make when struggling with their multiple losses. They need a safe secure environment that feels familiar. The decision is made without any guarantees but with much hope that because things can't get any worse, they will get better.

Our retirement in the desert ended within the following year after our sister-in-law's death. It wasn't a decision that was the result of our grief, but in looking back I can better understand how our grief was a large part of it. During the months following our sister-in-laws death, my wife's brother spoke about the possibility of moving out of Arizona. We both knew that it was because of family that we moved there in the first place. We also knew that our years there were missing something that we valued. Although we made some wonderful friends while we were there, we discovered that we shared no common history. Our roots in the desert, like some of the desert plants, were very shallow, while our deepest roots were back in the Midwest. We talked about where each other would move if one of us were to die, and we both agreed that we would move back to Columbus, Indiana where I had been the pastor of First Baptist Church for 12 years, and where our children had gone through school. We had put down our roots deeper in this town than anywhere else in our thirty-five years of pastoral ministry. We made our decision to move back while sitting on our patio and having coffee by our pool. It was an easy decision, but one that is difficult to explain to persons who can't imagine why anyone would move away from Arizona's blue sky and sunshine, for the Midwest humidity and snow. My only response is that it was not about the weather.

"Back home in Indiana" is more than a 'Hoosier' theme song; it is a phrase that describes the set-tled feeling we had upon returning together and not waiting for one of us to return alone. Naomi was returning home, and she was also fortunate not to have to return alone.

Personal Reflection
Have you ever returned to the familiar following a loss to redefine your hope? Was it all you hoped it would be? Were there disappointments?

Journal entry Six:
Beginning Again

I'm home now, and although I tell myself it's where I belong, I really don't feel much better. The village hasn't changed much and the old families are still here, but I am not the person I was when I left here. I've missed out on so much; it is hard to know how to begin again. Ruth came to me today and said she wanted to join the other women that she saw in the barley fields. She must be lonely away from her family. I know that feeling. I felt it when I moved to Moab. I know she wants to work so she can get on with her life and also help me. I appreciate her loving, willing spirit so I told her she could go to the barley fields if she wanted to. **N.**

It's difficult to begin again when all hope has been destroyed. Moving back to the familiar is no guarantee that a person will automatically feel better; however, the familiar surroundings may provide opportunities for new direction. Naomi had someone else to think about during this time and that provided her with the needed motivation to not sit around and have a pity party. She began to reinvest her energy in Ruth and introduce her to the culture and traditions of her people.

Personal Reflection
When has reinvesting your emotional energy in another person or project helped you?

It is this effort to see beyond one's personal emotional losses and take an interest in something or someone else that initiates beginning again. Persons may choose to involve themselves in volunteering or take on some new responsibility of helping a neighbor or family member. They have someone else on their minds and their energy is reinvested in them. *"The people I know who have most fully recovered their balance after a major loss are those who gave the most of themselves to others."* [2]

Naomi gave a lot of herself to Ruth. She offered guidance and help on how Ruth could move on with her life, and in the process, Naomi was moving on with her life also.

Journal entry seven:
God is so good.

This has been a wonderful day. What happened today has given me a renewed belief that God does care and take notice of our lives. Ruth came home all excited about meeting a man who not only allowed her to work in the barley fields, but he invited her to lunch and provided her with a special place to glean. She knows some of his servants even pulled some of the good standing sheaves and saw to it that she got them. When I asked her who this man was she said his name was Boaz. "Boaz", I said, "That's one of my husband's relatives! He's a wonderful man." She then told me all the details about the day and how good he was to her even though she was a foreigner. I advised her not to go to any other fields to work. Stay close to his servants. He will treat you well. N.

The journey of renewed hope will have its moments when the worry and anxiety of the past all seem so distant because something wonderful happens that wasn't even planned. Just about the time we are burdened with one more person telling us to 'have a nice day' we experience a serendipitous moment. We meet someone or hear some really good news that gives us renewed hope.

When we returned to Columbus to visit and look for housing, I scheduled a tour of the new fourteen bed hospice facility. The local hospice began in 1982 and I was their first volunteer chaplain while serving as a local church pastor, and I wanted to see their care facility. The executive director met me and asked me how long I would be in town. When I said, only for that day, but I also informed her of our decision to move back soon. She said, "Would you like a job?" She went on to explain that she had just had a meeting and she was given approval to hire a chaplain for the new facility. I quickly said yes, and three months later I began my chaplaincy with Hospice of South Central Indiana.

Such circumstances amaze us not only because it is good news, but because it wasn't something we would have dared to dream was possible. It's the kind of experience that many can't really appreciate without crediting it to a wonderful coincidence! When you have had such an experience, and have some appreciation for the faith values that have shaped life, you know the truth of the bumper sticker: *"Coincidence is God's way of remaining anonymous"*.

Personal Reflection
What unexpected serendipitous experience blessed your life and you knew it was no coincidence?

For Naomi, and for all who grieve, when that kind of moment comes, we begin to turn the corner that moves us out of the valley of the shadow and in the direction of a new day. Our anger at God over past circumstances that tore us apart and gave us reason to question God's fairness, are transformed into expressions of thanksgiving and praise. Naomi's words may just as well be our words at such a moment. *"Blessed be he by the Lord, whose kindness has not forsaken the living or the dead!"* (Ruth 2:20)

Journal entry Eight:
A Mother-in-law's advice

I am so excited about Boaz's interest in Ruth. Out of all the women who are working in the fields and those he has known all of these years, he has taken a liking to Ruth. I want the best for Ruth, and they don't get any better than Boaz. I've encouraged her not to let him get away. I even told her that if she wanted him, she needed to take some steps to letting him know her feelings. Tonight I told her he would be working late threshing the barley and she ought to go over and surprise him. I gave her some ideas about what to do. I hope it works out for her. **N.**

Getting involved in the lives of others doesn't leave much time to feel sorry for one's self. The more energy we expend hoping for the best to happen to others, transforms our own weariness and the burden becomes lighter. Being concerned about the happiness of another and feeling good about contributing to that happiness is part of what we must do to get outside our own grief and move on. At such a time it is not "our story" that is so important to tell, it is helping another write a new chapter in their story.

Journal entry Nine:
Hoping for the best

Ruth is such a dear daughter-in-law and I want the best for her. She told me all about last night and how Boaz treated her, and how he is such a gentleman and so respects the customs of our people that he doesn't want to do anything that isn't proper. Although he wants to have her as his own wife, he knows that there is another member of the family that must be considered first, and he insists on talking with him before he makes any commitment. I hope and pray that that this is meant to be. **N.**

Even when all seems to be going well in the journey toward a new future, there are moments when we are not in control of all of the circumstances. We will do our best to manipulate those circumstances to make events happen, but we are often confronted with a time of knowing it's not always up to us. It's the time of trusting and hoping that what we've come to value and appreciate. It is in these moments that we draw once again upon those faith values that have shaped us. We look back and see how far we have come and how good God has been, and we trust God for the future as well. Sometimes this period is only a day or two, and sometimes it may stretch on for months.

I know that there have been times in my ministry when I have been in that process of talking with search committees about a possible move, and I have had mixed degrees of investment in what I thought my future should be. When hoping for a specific decision that was in the hands of another, it was so important to keep a balanced outlook on the options the future held. Those were moments when the future was being defined by persons other than me.

Naomi must have felt that way about Boaz going to his relative to check out his interest in Ruth. The decision about their future, and to some degree Naomi's happiness, could be based on that decision.

The experience of redefining hope is not just a once and for all decision that moves us out of our grief and into a new day. It is a life time process that we continue to learn over and over again. Those times when circumstances are not within our control are the times when our faith is exercised and we grow in our awareness that there is One outside ourselves to whom we look for guidance.

Journal entry Ten: O Happy Day!

It's been years since I wrote my last entry, and so much has happened. The community gave Boaz the blessing to take Ruth as his wife. The blessing was for them to bear children and establish a name in Bethlehem. I was surprised, not at the acceptance of our people of Ruth, a foreigner, but by the blessing that they gave me. They affirmed that God had not left me, and when their baby Obed was born they placed him in my arms as if I were the mother. I could not help but think about Elimelech and about Mahlon my son, Ruth's first husband. Those were bittersweet years out of which I have come to know God cares for me even when I am angry at him. Then I could not have dreamed of this day back home in Bethlehem, with Ruth and Boaz, holding their baby Obed in my arms. **N.**

If we could only remember the lessons we have learned looking in the rear view mirror; lessons of how we managed to redefine our hope in seemingly hopeless situations. I cannot help but wonder how many tears are in God's bottle labeled 'Naomi'?

Journal entry Eleven:
A Post Script

I am the wife of Jesse, my father-in-law Obed gave me this journal. It has told me much of our genealogy and I just want to add my word of gratitude. Jesse and I, like other family members still live here in Bethlehem. We now have eight sons. Our youngest son was just born and we named him David. **Nitzevet** [3]

Little did Naomi know that as she struggled with her grief and worked at redefining her hope, that her decisions would not only shape her family, but would one day be part of redefining the hope for the world?

To some degree each person's effort at redefining hope will have a life-changing effect, not only on them, but on generations which follow.

Chapter 4

Sherry Redefines Her Hope

It was early morning and her room was still dark. She was admitted to our hospice facility the evening before, and as the chaplain, I always attempt to meet newly admitted patients as soon as possible. I walked into the room so I could see if she was awake, and when I looked, I could see that her eyes were open. She saw me, and said, "Come, in I'm awake."

I have learned from patients that some of their loneliest times are during the night or before dawn when they have not been able to sleep, and no one is there. It is therefore a good time for a person to show up and be with them. Sitting by the bedside at such an unusual time often creates a special atmosphere for persons knowing someone really cares about them, and it helps them in some way to share what it is they are thinking and feeling.

She said, "Please come in, I've been awake for some time."

I walked to her bedside, slid the folding chair close to the head of the bed, extended my hand to hers and told her I was the chaplain, and I hoped I wasn't intruding on any special quiet time she might have been having. She indicated I was not and that I was indeed welcome.

She said, "My name's Sherry, and you are an answer to my prayers."

I smiled and asked, "Would you mind sharing with me what you mean by that?"

She continued, "Now that my cancer has reached this stage, and I know there's nothing more I can do, I need to talk about some things."

"Tell me how you know there's nothing more you can do?"

"I've been a nurse for 23 years... I've worked in oncology and my doctors have given me all the available treatments... and I'm in hospice because there will be no cure."

Personal Reflection
Have you ever heard a medical report "There's nothing more we can do"? Describe how you felt.

She then proceeded to tell me about her journey of nearly five years when she was first diagnosed, and how she went into remission and went back to work, not as a nurse, but in the office. She told me how supportive her fellow employees, her husband, and her two sons had been. She told about the cancer reappearing and for the last year she had been receiving treatments until the news yesterday that there was nothing more anyone could do. Even with the dimly lit room, I could see a reflection of light bouncing off a tear that had rolled to her cheek. I reached out and put my hand on top of hers and asked, "And how am I the answer to your prayer?"

She said, "I've never been baptized, and I would like to be, but I'm afraid it is too late now."

There was such sadness in her tone of voice as she shared the hopelessness of the news that there were no more treatments possible, and then the despair of concluding that she had put off being baptized until now and now it was too late.

"Would you tell me about your spiritual journey," I inquired, "and what brings you to this desire?"

She then began telling me about herself and her husband Mike and how they were married in his church and began attending regularly. After about a year she felt like she would like to join the church and she signed up for the membership class. She said she went through all the classes and at the end a date was set and those in the class were to be in the worship service where they would be welcomed into the church membership. She confessed to being too new and too shy to raise her concern about baptism, so she just went along with the others. They were in the church for many years, had their two sons baptized there and later moved out of the community, but never found another church they wanted to attend.

"I just don't feel complete without being baptized", she confessed.

"Sherry, let me reassure you that we can take care of that any time you choose. You just tell me when you would like to be baptized and I will arrange for it right here in your room, even while you are in your bed."

A smile crossed her face, and she said, "Oh, I would love that...and I want my husband to be here with me. He's having a real hard time accepting this, and I want you to meet him. Could we do it this evening when he comes here after work?"

"You tell me the time", I responded, "and I will be here and we'll have a baptism."

"He said he would come right from work and get here about 5:45."

"Well, I'll be here at 6:00 to meet him, and to share in your baptism", I promised.

"Thank you so much" she said, as she stretched out both arms and I leaned in so she could hug me.

I shared a prayer with her before I left, again promising her I would be back at 6:00 that evening.

This first visit with Sherry reinforced what other patients have taught me about the hopelessness and despair a person feels when they are told by the doctor "There's nothing more we can do." The hopelessness creates a sadness that unleashes uncontrollable tears. These tears at this time are the tears the Psalmist says God collects in a bottle. In these precious moments of coming to terms with such hopeless news, God knows all about the sadness and reassures us that our tears do not go unnoticed.

For Sherry, the sadness and hopelessness was compounded by regret that she had not done what she knew God's Word had taught her she ought to do and that was to be baptized as a sign that she was a child of God. Those tears she shed over her neglect, God also collected, and God also heard the desire of her heart.

I sense the same hopelessness in others that I meet who also sign on for our hospice services. At such a time my role as chaplain is to help them redefine their hope for whatever time they may have remaining. When I ask a patient who has shared such a sense of hopelessness with me, "What are you hoping for now?", they look at me with a blank stare as if I didn't hear all they had just told me about how hopeless their situation was. I find I have to repeat myself and also explain myself so they will be able to understand the seriousness of my question.

Once they hear me explain how they have the opportunity to be hopeful, even with a limited amount of time available, they begin to show a change of facial expression which I define as the beginning of redefining their hope. Only they can identify who it is that they want to see or what it is they want to do before they die. When specific hopes are identified and are within the realm of being possible, they discover that they do have something to live for, and that gives them reason to look forward to tomorrow.

For Sherry, I heard her hope and it was not that she would somehow have a miraculous recovery, but that before she died she could be baptized. It is a privilege to be the person who is invited to join another on this end-of-life journey, and to be part of their process of redefining their hope. I also heard Sherry hope that her husband Mike would be able to accept the reality of the disease so they could be on the same page that enabled them to talk and plan.

That evening, I arrived at Sherry's room a few minutes before six. I had a very special bowl of cut glassware, as well as a baptismal certificate. I had prepared a sign for the door and informed the staff so that no one would interrupt the baptism. I entered and met Mike and provided a meaningful personal experience of baptism for Sherry. Mike and Sherry both had tears in their eyes, and these tears were not so much because of the sadness of the moment, but because of the joy of a fulfilled hope that they both knew was important for Sherry. God collects our tears of joy as well. The moment was so special when I left I told them it might be good to just keep the sign on the door for a while so they could talk. They agreed.

The next morning when I saw Sherry, she was all smiles and eager to share with me how she and Mike had spent nearly an hour talking and how he finally shared that he knew this was the end, but he didn't want to have her think he had given up hope. She told him neither one had to give up hope; they just had to hope together.

I said, "What is it you are hoping for together?"

She said, "We hope I can get out of here and return home and we can both start to go to church together again." She then asked, "What church do you go to?"

I told her and she had this very positive attitude that she wanted to attend there also. I knew they lived over 25 miles from the church and didn't really seriously think that would happen until one Sunday morning several weeks later when I saw them walk past the pew I was sitting in, and sit down three pews in front of me. She was carrying her portable oxygen, and he was helping her with her walker. They attended for several months until she had a set back and was brought back to our inpatient critical care facility.

After several days when she had regained her strength and was able to converse we talked again about her hopes, and she said she didn't think she was going to make it to June to see her youngest son graduate from high school. She was resigned to knowing that was just too far away given how she now felt. She shared this regret not only with our staff but with some of her former nurses who came daily to see her. One of them suggested to our staff that we might want to consider checking with her son's high school principal and see if an early graduation could be held for her son in our facility. When we talked with her husband about this he agreed that it was a good idea and he would call the principal.

The arrangements were made with the high school for the principal and the son's counselor to come on a certain day at a certain time and bring the cap and gown and diploma. Our staff prepared the patient's patio outside with decorations, provided a cake, ice cream and punch, and her son's graduation ceremony was held two months early. Pictures were taken, and an article was written for the local newspaper, and a family's hope had been fulfilled.

She actually was able to return home again and attend church for a couple of Sundays before being brought back into our facility. I remember going in to see her on a Wednesday morning and she was feeling very sad, with tears in her eyes and I was surprised because I had commended them on their wonderful experiences of fulfilled hopes. I asked her, "Sherry, what's happening, why the sadness?"

She said, "I was planning on going forward this Sunday at church so I could join, but that's not going to happen." The tears she shed were tears of hopelessness over something desired, but never to be experienced. The disease had reached a new level of robbing her of strength, and in that weakness she drew her hopeless conclusion.

I offered to contact the pastor and share this hope with him and see what he might be able to do about it, and she appeared somewhat hopeful as she said that would be fine. I made the contact and the pastor visited with Sherry and Mike and explained that the following Sunday a group of persons would be welcomed into membership and if she would like he would add her name. She quickly agreed. The following Sunday the pastor introduced all of those present who were joining, and then read Sherry's name and told of her faith journey, church attendance, and her hope of joining on that Sunday but was in the hospice facility. He shared that he would visit her the following day and he would welcome her as a new member.

Monday morning at 9:00 the pastor arrived at the facility. Sherry had failed, but was still alert and able to recognize those who were present. Her husband and I joined with the pastor at the bedside as the pastor not only welcomed her into member-ship but served each of us the bread and wine of the body and blood of Christ. It was a precious moment, especially for me as it had been my privilege to share this six month hope filled journey of baptism, graduation, church attendance and membership, and a final communion together. The tears God collected from me that morning were because of the joy of sharing such a sacred journey. Two days later Sherry died.

Patients have taught me over and over again the power of hope. When a terminally ill person redefines their hope they unleash that power and are amazed at what their future holds. A future not measured in years or even months, but in tangible hopes and dreams that make the end of life meaningful, not only for them but also for those who hope with them.

Personal Reflection
Have you had an experience where you witnessed the power of hope? Have you seen it in another who faced the end of life? How were you part of their story?

Chapter 5

JOB
His Final Conversation with His Hospice Chaplain

It has been my privilege to have been a hospice chaplain and to have journeyed with persons who are dying. Hospice chaplains offer dying patients the option of doing a life review, so that they will be able to express and affirm the meaning of those spiritual values by which they have lived. By asking a person questions, which invites them to reflect upon their life's journey, they are able to share themselves with another, and in doing so they discover how meaningful life has been. It is a privilege to listen and be with them as they journey back in time and revisit the joys and sorrows that define their story. There are times when their story includes some unfinished business. By asking questions that invite reflection, the dying patients are able to choose what is most important for them to share.

I have imagined what it might have been like to have been a chaplain for Job, and had the privilege of sharing a final conversation with him. What follows is an imaginary dialogue of Job's final conversation with his hospice chaplain before he died.

Job is being cared for in a hospice care facility.

It is daybreak. Light begins to illuminate the room. As a chaplain I have had some of my best conversations with patients at the beginning of the day before the breakfast tray or family members arrive. Upon entering the room I see the patient is awake, his eyes are open.

Chaplain: "Good morning, Job"

Job: "Good morning, chaplain. You're up bright and early."

Chaplain: I opened the folding chair and set it near the bed, "I thought this might be a good time for us to talk. I hope you had a restful night."

Job: "I slept well. It's good to see you."

Chaplain: "We have some unfinished business. If you remember my last visit, I asked you to think about your life and those experiences which shaped your spiritual values."

There was a period of silence as I sat down and I was able to look him in the eyes. He took a deep breath, nodded his head, and slowly spoke.

Job: "I've given that a lot of thought." (More silence) "I'm not quite sure where to begin... I've known great joy and I've had tragic sorrow."

Chaplain: "Are you willing to share some of it with me?"

Job: "Well, I was very fortunate and blessed. My wife and I had seven sons and three daughters and we owned a very large farm. Our livestock included thousands of sheep and camels, and hundreds of oxen and donkeys. We had servants that managed it all. Life was good, but then tragedy struck. Up until then I really hadn't ever lost anything or experienced any circumstances that I didn't feel I couldn't overcome." He pauses and reflects and I'm not sure he's going to continue, so I ask,

Chaplain: "What is it you lost?"

Job: "Everything… my livestock and servants were stolen or killed; my sons and daughters were having a party at my eldest son's house when a tornado destroyed the house and they all died. Everything I had worked for…everything I had valued was gone in one day. It was just my wife and me."

Chaplain: "I can't begin to imagine what that must have been like. How did you ever get through such a difficult time?"

Job: "Well, I've always been a religious man, and I've always given God the credit for everything I had. God had truly blessed me. As bad as I felt and as sad as I was, I knew I had to turn to God. I had often wondered what I would do if I lost everything that mattered to me. At such moments I simply told myself that since God had given it all to me, God could also take it from me... remembering that didn't make it any easier, but my mind kept trying to talk my heart into believing that. I performed the proper religious rituals in an effort to express my grief and sorrow. It's what I knew I should do, so I did it, but I'm not sure my heart was in it."

Chaplain: "Why do you say that?"

Job: "It wasn't long before I began to break out in hives all over my body and I was very miserable. What made me a bit angry was my wife didn't help the matter any."

Chaplain: "In what way?"

Job: "To her, my physical torment with the hives was the last straw and she suggested I curse God and die and be relieved of my misery. That's not what I needed to hear, because I knew there was some truth in what she was saying."

Chaplain: "What truth is that?"

Job: "There are times when I have felt like death would be the best way out from the suffering and sorrow, and that was one of those times. Hearing her say that just increased my anxiety because I knew in my mind that was not an option if I really trusted God. I told myself that the hives and sores were my fault for not really fully trusting God."

Personal Reflection
Have you ever reasoned that way about your life circumstances, tragedy or matters of health?

Chaplain: "If your wife wasn't much support, where did you find any support to help you get through such a trying time?"

Job: "To be honest with you, I didn't know where to turn. One day when I was feeling my worst...looking back now I know I was in a deep depression...I had long periods of time when

I couldn't stop sobbing. That's when my three friends showed up to comfort me. I guess word got around that 'ole Job was having a pity party so they felt they should make an appearance and help me."

Chaplain: "And were they helpful?"

Job: With a sarcastic kind of grin he replied, "At times I thought they were, and at times I wished they would have never come."

Chaplain: "How were they helpful?"

Job: "When they arrived and saw me in such a depressed state of mind, I think my appearance overwhelmed them and no doubt shocked them and they began to wail and cry, and then they sat with me in silence for a whole week. I later realized that was very helpful."

Personal Reflection
Have you ever experienced a friend showing up at just the right time to share your grief? Was it helpful?

Chaplain: "Why was that?"

Job: "I couldn't explain it to anyone. I just felt that having them share tears together with me, and stay with me for the whole week somehow reminded me that someone cared about me. However, it didn't take away my sorrow, my sores or my anger. After about a week, I had had enough and I blew it. I cursed the day I was born. I went on and on about how I felt. It was the first time I was able to verbalize my feelings, and when I finished I felt a bit better...that was until my friend Eliphaz had to scold me for being so impatient and not practicing what I had preached to others."

Chaplain: "What I hear you saying is that wasn't very helpful."

Job: "That's exactly what I'm saying. If there was anything I didn't need right then, it was a sermon. I had just begun to have the courage to risk telling my friends how I was feeling, and then I get the message, 'Don't feel that way'... or 'you deserve to feel that way because...' That's not what I wanted to hear, and I'm afraid I lost it."

Personal Reflection
At a time of loss/grief have you ever had another tell you or imply that you should "get over it"?

Chaplain: "What do you mean you 'lost it'?"

Job: "I tore into my friend by unloading a lot more feelings than I intended to...maybe in looking back, that wasn't a bad thing, but at the time he upset me with his pious lecture. It made me just want God to take my life and get it over with. I didn't feel I could deal with my troubles or my friend any longer."

Chaplain: "What about the other two friends, were they any more helpful?"

Job: "Not a bit. As a matter of fact, they piled on and did much of the same. Each of them had their own favorite cliché's and religious advice which was intended to make me feel better. It evolved into a debate, and it was three against one. When Bildad and Zophar added their two cents worth, I gave it right back to them. Elihu, another young friend, showed up and he had advice also. I grew weary listening, but I remained firm in my conviction regarding my integrity and my innocence. I needed God to make himself known and I struggled as to why God seemed to be so unfair and so distant. I have to say that through all the arguing and debating I began to feel better."

Personal Reflection
Why would Job feel better after arguing with his friends? Have you found "letting it out" expressing your true feelings has helped?

Chaplain: "Was there some turning point when you began to experience peace, and have a renewed confidence in God?"

Job: "Yes. I don't remember if it was a dream or vision, but I knew God was speaking to me and finally getting through to me. I guess I was so wrapped up in my own little world of trials and troubles that I had talked a lot about my God who was in charge, but I really failed to see the bigger picture of just how much in charge he is."

Chaplain: "What was that dream or vision that helped you see the bigger picture?"

Job: "I don't know if I can begin to describe it to you. In some wonderful way I was able to see the world from God's perspective. It was as though I was out there with God and God was pointing out just how he created it all. In the conversation we were having he was asking the questions... questions for which God knew I had no answers...big questions like, 'Where were you when I created this world?' 'Do you know who has cut a channel for the torrents of rain?' 'Who has wisdom to number the clouds?' I felt so little. In feeling so little, I saw my sorrow and grief in the much larger perspective of how our Creator God sees our world. It was awesome, and I finally came to accept my life and all the unwanted circumstances because I was reassured that God was going to provide for all of my needs."

Personal Reflection
Have you had a similar spiritual insight which marked a turning point in your experience?

Chaplain: "And how has God provided for all your needs since then?"
Job: "God has blessed me with more than I could have ever imagined. It's as though God has doubled all the blessings I had before my sorrow. God has blessed me with family... I have great grandchildren who are such a blessing...I have livestock and servants...the farm has become more than I could have ever dreamed. God is so good, and I am ready to die now a blessed man and not an angry man."
Chaplain: "Thank you, Job. Your life has been a blessing and an example, not only for your family, but for the family of God. Let me offer a prayer of thanks for your life.

Job's story is also our story. Our story includes having to face the unwanted circumstances of life where we lose what we value so dearly and experience a grief that we are convinced no one else understands.

We, like Job, have continued to practice our religious rituals as a means of holding on to the spiritual thread of faith hoping God will not forget us.

We, like Job, have felt no one knows how we feel, not even the closest of family members who in their own way wish we could just 'get over it'.

We, like Job, have friends who mean well, but offer cliché's that are empty and only increase our anger and frustration.

We, like Job, have been brought to a place where we finally see the larger perspective and are able to proceed on with our grief work toward acceptance.

We, like Job, are able to hear the reassuring words that our God who was there collecting Job's tears, is here now, and will also collect ours.

Chapter 6

"When Johnny Comes Marching Home Again..."

The risk of asking questions that invite reflection is that the one asking gives up control of the conversation, and does not know what the dying person might say. All too often persons who visit the dying want to avoid having the patient have to think or talk about issues that might bring tears or sadness. Tears risk creating an uncomfortable tension between persons. The avoidance of such questions indicates a level of discomfort in handling another's emotions.

Personal Reflection

Have you ever intentionally avoided a topic with another who was going through a difficult time because you didn't want them to get emotional? Have you had others avoid a topic with you?

One morning I entered an 84 year old patient's room and noticed the patient was awake and staring at the ceiling. This was my second visit with this man. I was asked to see him by our medical director because the patient had shown restlessness that medications were not helping to control. When that happens, there is often a spiritual need that is causing the discomfort, and those who deal with the physical symptoms of the dying know the importance of addressing the spiritual needs as well.

I sat in the chair next to the bed, reached over and placed my hand on his. We sat in silence for a minute or two, and then I asked him, "When you are here alone, what is it you think about most?"

He gave a slight squeeze to my hand, and in his slow deliberate speech while still looking at the ceiling he said, "I killed three men."

It was not a response that I expected, and I could tell by his mood he was very sad. I noticed tears beginning to form in his eyes. I said, "Are you able to tell me about that?"

"I had to do it, it was either them or me", he replied as he appeared to be reliving the anguish of that moment.

"Where were you, and how did it happen?" I asked.

"It was during the war and we were in France...sniper fire was coming in on our company, and my buddies were being shot. (silence) I had to do it; it was either them or me... (Silence and tears, as I waited for him to proceed) I could see where the snipers were holed up just above me on a ridge. They couldn't see me, but I could see them...I killed all three of them... when the shooting stopped most of my buddies were dead... then I climbed the ridge and made sure they were dead. They were just young boys like me. I had to do it; it was either them or me."

His tears increased as he breathed deeply seemingly relieved that he had finally told his story to someone. I squeezed his hand gently and called him by name saying, "It was either their country or our country. Thank you for your service. I can't begin to imagine how hard that must have been, or how awful you have felt all these years, but I can assure you that you only did what was necessary under those circumstances. You are one of the "Greatest Generation" that has enabled America to be free. Thank you."

He looked at me, and squeezed my hand, and said, "I hope God will forgive me."

I assured him that our God was a forgiving God, and that his actions so long ago on behalf of his country have provided the freedom we enjoy today. I affirmed his value of human life, and his sensitivity to carrying out his military duty and reminded him that God knew the desires of his heart. It was my privilege to provide the assurance and peace that calmed his restlessness.

After a period of silence I asked him if I could offer a prayer to God thanking God for the forgiveness God offers, and the service he and his buddies gave. He agreed. I left that room and my final conversation with him believing that he had lived all these years bearing that pain and never sharing it with anyone. I could not help but wonder if the heroic welcome given to the soldiers returning from war also was a signal for them not to shed any tears over what they had to do. Yet how many have had to live with deeds done that have never been shared, but carried as burdens to the grave. It was his unfinished business, and giving him the opportunity to reflect on his life enabled him to find peace, and to have another affirm his heroic contribution to his country. Two days later, he died.

Dying patients continue to teach me the importance of taking care of "unfinished business" before the end. The difficulty is having someone who will risk asking the open ended questions that will allow the dying to share their tears and whatever is on their minds. Such a question sends a signal to the dying that we are there for them, and we are willing to listen to their stories. In the telling of their stories we may hear them express their hope.

When he got to the end of his story and almost as an afterthought expressed his hope that God would forgive him, he was finally putting into words the issue that had caused his restlessness. His troubled soul wrestled for years with the idea that his God might not be big enough to forgive him. How reassuring to know that when forgiveness and peace are requested, and when tears are shed, God has been there all the time waiting to collect them.

Personal Reflection
Can you think of other open ended questions that show your sincere interest while encouraging them to share their story?

Chapter 7

A Grief Walk

Luke 24:13-24

This story in Luke 24 is the familiar story of the two Emmaus disciples walking home from Jerusalem the week following the crucifixion of Jesus. The story has meant many things to many people and has even been used as a model for an organization that provides experiences of solitude and reflection for Christians. If a person has been on an "Emmaus Walk", then they have experienced one of these meaningful spiritual encounters.

As important as those encounters are for persons today, when I read the story of that first century walk that the disciples made I understand the importance of it as a resurrection appearance account, but we must not lose sight of the fact that it begins as a grief journey. It is numbered among the many grief stories throughout the Bible that illustrate what grief looked like in the lives of those who followed God. When we examine the dialogue of these two disciples and imagine their emotions, we have insight into these men who were processing their grief and redefining their hope.

We who read Luke's account, know the story so well that we are tempted to rush to its resurrection conclusion and miss the circumstances of sorrow and grief that define the emotions of the disciples. They are walking back to their home after being in Jerusalem and experiencing the horror of crucifixion. It wasn't just another Roman crucifixion that troubled them; it was a crucifixion of someone they knew. The person wasn't just a family member or close friend. The person was the prophet who they had hoped would redeem Israel. They were walking home and talking about what happened. They were fortunate to have had each other to share a common grief where the understanding each others deep feelings of loss. They were able to verbalize how they felt about all the things that had happened that weekend. They must have surely had their questions: "How could this have happened?" "Why did this happen?"

Having a stranger join them on their walk home, must have been a common occurrence. People would join others and travel together if for no other reason than for safety. Their conversation no doubt continued as they were deep into their grief and searching for some way to make sense out of their sorrow. The stranger listened and then asked them what they were talking about. They are shocked that anyone coming from Jerusalem didn't know what happened.

I can imagine the same kind of reaction the day following 9/11/01 in New York City after the airplanes destroyed the twin towers of the World Trade Center. It would have been hard to believe there was someone in town who hadn't heard the awful news. The two grief stricken travelers were dumbfounded by the stranger's lack of information regarding the crucifixion. It seems they couldn't even bring themselves to use the word crucifixion and had to speak in more general terms about the "things that had taken place".

Persons who grieve often cannot bring themselves to use the words death, died, or killed and substitute more generic words like passed away, accident, or gone. It is an indication of their level of sorrow and their desire to maintain emotional control. What a person needs at such a time is exactly what the two grief travelers received; a person who will journey with them and allow them to process their story of loss.

Personal Reflection
Can you remember a grief experience when you had someone with you to allow you to pour out your feelings? Remember how that felt?

The stranger, turned grief counselor simply asked "What things?" and this provided the invitation to verbalize the story of their loss and the reason for their sorrow. Helping others who are grieving is as simple as asking the right questions which encourage the person grieving to expand on their feelings of loss. Such questions keep the focus on the other's grief, and resist the temptation to insert a personal grief story. All too often when a grieving person begins to share their story, the listener quickly responds with their own experience of grief, thinking they are identifying with the feelings of the person grieving, but they are simply focusing on a safe story that they can control. This transfer of focus signals the one grieving that the listener isn't really interested in the emotions that may be shared.

One of the key phrases in this story is, "*We* **had** *"hoped"* and all the circumstances described in the story describe for us just how great was their loss, sorrow, and disappointment. They were going back home, back to the familiar to pick up the pieces. The road to Emmaus is their grief journey. On their journey they were provided with a way to rethink their loss in light of a larger perspective. They were reminded that their spirituality held the secret for them to process their grief. They were reminded what the Prophets had said. In hearing and remembering they were able to get outside the emotion of their grief and see the bigger picture. As they processed that in their discussion they began to redefine their hope. The process they went through illustrates what Paul wrote about when he said, *"We do not grieve as others do who have no hope."* (1 Thessalonians 4:13)

The spirituality of hope begins to be redefined in the midst of our grief.

What Jesus did for them was unique in that he personally enabled them to process their grief until their "eyes were opened", until their attitude was changed to the possibilities of a new future. I want to suggest to you that people today, like you and me, are able to help others move beyond their grief and have their eyes opened to a new future. Although grief work is very personal, it is not necessarily done in isolation. We need others, whether we are in a support group or one on one with a good friend, to provide us with a loving caring presence that finds ways of helping us begin to see the larger perspective.

A box of dominoes is a wonderful metaphor [1] that illustrates how a loving caring presence helps a grieving person.

Imagine being in a room with another person and that person is holding a box of dominoes. As the person turns to speak to you their dominoes box suddenly spills. All of their dominoes are scattered everywhere on the floor. The person who spilled their dominoes is stunned, shocked, surprised by the turn of events. He stands and stares at his dominoes. Your immediate reaction is to stoop and start picking up the dominoes and putting them back in the empty box. You want to help, but there is no possible way you can put the dominoes back in the order they were before they spilled. There was an order to the dominoes only known by the one who owned them. Each domino represented some portion of the person's life; their family, job, friends, and spiritual beliefs, just to name just a few. Only that person can put them where they belong, and to do so will take some time. Only that person can choose if they even want to put some of them back or if they might choose to live without them. During that time the person will find it helpful to have you with them, not to speed up their process, but to simply reassure them that you are there if you can help in any way.

This is the loving presence that Jesus provided for the disciples who were grieving. His interest in them and the conversation he had with them enabled them to realign their 'dominoes' in a way that redefined their hope. It is in providing this kind of loving caring relationship that we are able to help grieving persons have their "eyes opened" to new possibilities.

Personal Reflection
Who is that one person that comes to mind that was most helpful to you at a time of grief? Why is that person special?

There is an element of time that passes that is important to this story. We who read the story know that it is a seven mile walk from Jerusalem to Emmaus. Given their state of mind and the thoughtful dialogue they were having a twenty minute mile would be a pretty good pace, if so, it would have taken them about two and one-half hours. The distance between

Jerusalem and Emmaus represents the passage of time and that is important. Grief work takes time.

Personal Reflection
Think of a past grief and draw a time-line with the date of its beginning on the left and today's date on the right. Can you divide that time into periods that identify the progress of your journey? Can you name who has been helpful?

We see how during the passing of time that the disciples spirituality transformed their attitude and because of their reaching out and inviting the stranger to eat with them, they began the process of reinvesting their energy in another. When the moment of truth hit them, they reflected back on their journey and began to piece together their movement toward acceptance and a new hope. They expressed their reflection in the words, *"Were not our hearts burning within us while he was talking to us on the road....*" (Luke 24:32) Helping another who is grieving to redefine hope is a time consuming process.

It will do no good to tell the grieving person, *"One day you will understand."* Such understanding comes only through the personal experience of the grieving person. Based on the level of emotional investment that has been lost, they determine the length of that process.

When we reflect on our own personal past grief experiences of how we processed our sorrow and sadness, we ought to be able to identify some moment, some turning point when the element of hope began to help us shape a new future; a future, which did not forget the loss, but incorporated the loss into a new way of living.

Personal Reflection
On your previous time-line can you mark that period when your hope began to feel possible?

The Emmaus story ends with the wonderful awareness of a resurrected Jesus, and the two who grieved so deeply find a new energy for living. They were excited enough to invest that energy in running seven miles back to Jerusalem to tell their friends. Good news must be shared, and they must have assumed that their story of grief and sorrow was also being experienced by others, and they needed to be there for them.

This Emmaus disciple story has become a vital part of the truths and teachings that are part of the Christian's spiritual heritage. Of the many lessons this story of resurrection faith teaches one, we must not overlook the hope of beginning again after experiencing sorrow and grief.

Chapter 8

The Power of 'With'

There are two financial institutions which have become partners and to advertise their merger they have made their advertising campaign "The Power of 'With'". They use various images and messages to underscore how important and powerful it is to experience the human connection 'with' another.

Personal Reflection
Can you think of a time in your life when you discovered how important it is having someone "With you"?

As a small child, our family would go and visit our aunt and uncle who lived up in the Allegheny Mountains where they didn't have indoor plumbing or electric lights. I have fond memories of our visits there. One memory taught me the power of "with. " After a long day of playing outdoors with my cousins, our family would sit together in the parlor and I would fall asleep on a daybed set up in that room. Sometime during the middle of the night, I would wake up and begin to cry because I was afraid of the dark. Because it was in the mountains and there was no electricity, there were no night lights or street lights and it was so dark I could not even see my hand in front of my face. As I cried I would feel someone sit on the edge of my bed and begin to pat me on the arm telling me it will be okay. My mother's voice was reassuring me that I was not alone and she was 'with' me. That made all the difference in my world during the darkness. She did not try to calm me by explaining the number of hours which remained before the sun would come up, or the promise of something future that would distract me from my fears. She just sat on the bed and patted my shoulders and rubbed my back and I soon fell asleep. I was content that she was with me. Those facing the end of their lives, desire this same comfort.

The sign on the patient's door said, "No Visitors". As the hospice chaplain, I didn't think that meant me, but I checked with the patient's nurse just to be sure. She told me that the patient did want me to continue visiting, along with one friend named Fran, but no one else.

I quietly entered the patient's room and sat in the available chair next to the bedside. She opened her eyes, and smiled, and I asked her if she would like me to share a devotional reading with her. She nodded that she would like that.

For the past three weeks, I had been visiting with Janet, a 54 year old, and at her request reading scripture, a devotional, and offering a prayer. Janet was not married and I knew that she had a limited number of family members, two nieces did visit nearly every day. In my mind I wondered how they would feel when they saw the sign, or were told by the nurse that they could not visit. I also wondered why Janet would make such a request.

I shared my devotional reading and thoughts and offered a prayer. I could see she was appreciative of the spiritual support, but was nearing the end of life and not having a lot of energy to carry on a conversation. Before I left, I asked if she would mind telling me why she had requested the "No Visitors" sign be put on her door.

In her quiet gentle manner, speaking slowly and deliberately she said, "The people who visit me do a lot of meaningless jabbering about things that I have no interest in, and it makes me tired. I even close my eyes and pretend to be asleep so they will leave. I'd rather not have them here."

I told her I understood that and affirmed her decision, but then asked her, "But, you have made one exception for a friend named Fran. Why is it important that she be allowed to visit if the others are restricted?"

Janet again gave me a gentle smile and proceeded to say, "Well, you have to know Fran to appreciate her. She comes in and slides the easy chair over here by the bedside, and sits down. She asks if there's anything I need, and when I tell her 'no' she just sits with me by my bedside. She doesn't try to carry on a conversation with me, she's just with me. After two or three hours she says her goodbyes and leaves." Tears began to show at the corner of her eyes as she continued, "I can't begin to tell you how much it means to me for her to just be here with me. Sometimes I doze off, but when I awaken, she's right here with me."

Personal Reflection
Have you ever had someone gift you by being with you at a special time in your life?

Janet knew and appreciated the power of 'with' which Fran practiced. It is a principle that appears so simple on the surface; you just have to show up and sit with another, and that person feels at peace. However, it is a principle that few people are comfortable practicing because we live in a culture that has conditioned us to be busy. We live in a society that values a work ethic of "doing for" as opposed to "being with". Being with often implies silence, and silence isn't always 'golden'; but sometimes very threatening. It is the silence that creates an uncomfortable feeling that persons deal with by talking, and the talking is often meaningless chatter which means little to the person who is dying. It is usually about what is happening in their world, and not what is being experienced in the world of the one who is facing the end of life. Janet's visitors were limited in what they could "do" for her, so as a substitute for doing, they kept the silence at a distance by their constant 'jabbering'.

There is no more difficult visit than 'with' an Alzheimer's patient who speaks words and phrases, but is unable to connect them to communicate. When I sit 'with' such a person there are often long periods of silence between us. I wait for a moment that feels appropriate to introduce some familiar spiritual religious ritual. One morning, I sat with such a patient I had known for just over a year, holding her right hand, and at the right time I affirmed God's love for the patient and shared with her the Lord's Prayer. She bowed her head, eyes open, and when I finished and said amen, she moved her left hand to cover our hands and looking at me she said, "I believe that." Then she leaned in toward me and said 'kiss', so I turned my cheek and she kissed me, and I kissed her on the forehead. As I drew back she said, "I love you." I believe that such a brief moment of connecting comes from time spent 'with' another where there is a spirit to spirit connection.

I do not want to imply that 'being with' is easy. I will be the first to confess my frustrations when visiting a dementia patient. Since I believe the dying are our best teachers, I often ask myself what it is I learn from this frustration, and then one day as I was leaving such a visit it dawned on me. My frustration comes from knowing how important feedback is in any relationship. When a relationship is one-sided and only one party is giving, the giver gets discouraged and it isn't long before there is no longer a relationship. Meaningful relationships are a mixture of giving and receiving. The particular patient I was visiting the day I discovered this was a person who, during my previous four visits, had never looked at me, and never spoken to me. He sat looking at the television. No matter what I attempted, I was not able to solicit any kind of response. On this particular day, my fifth visit, he was looking at the pictures in a magazine on his tray table. I sat with him and made comments about the animals and the scenery he was observing. I wondered how much of what he was looking at he was processing, and then I noticed that there were times when he accidently turned more than one page and when he did he stopped and backed up the page so he didn't miss any of the pictures. He did this often as we went through two magazines. I was convinced that he was able to process information, so when I stood to leave and tell him goodbye, I put my hand out for a departing handshake. He looked at it for about fifteen seconds then lifted his hand off of the tray table and grasped mine, and as he did he looked at me and he squeezed my hand in a firm grip. I responded with my own firm grip and said, "Thank you, I'll see you next week."

Leaving his room gave me such a good feeling because for the first time he gave me something back. I can't be sure what he intended to communicate to me, but I want to believe that the firmness and the look was his "thank you" to me for just being with him.

Joseph's greatest consolation was that he continually claimed the truth that his God was with him, and would provide for him. In the story of Naomi, the power of 'with' is seen as Ruth stays with Naomi as she makes the difficult grief journey home. Job is most comforted by his friends during the first days of their visit with him when they sat in silence. They spoiled their effort when they opened their mouths and started explaining everything, and attempted to answer the unanswerable. The two Emmaus disciples were open to a new perspective because a stranger journeys "with them".

The biblical teaching of God being "with us" is at the very heart of the Judeo-Christian teachings. It is what is learned from the stories of Israel's Journey out of Egypt, through the wilderness, and into the Promised Land. It is taught in the symbols of the ark as well as the tent and tabernacle, the cloud by day and pillar of fire by night. It is evident in Daniel's lion's den as well as Nebuchadnezzar's fiery furnace and in the Valley of the Shadow of death where there is a Shepherd with the sheep. The importance of the power of 'with' is underscored by God, when the Son of God is given the name "Emmanuel", meaning 'God is with us'. It is a presence that provides the most comfort and peace at the times when our tears flow freely and God collects them in a bottle.

Personal Reflection
When has another's presence "with you" reassured you of God's presence?

Chapter 9

David Learns to Grieve Well

Grief education is a life-long process, and no biblical character illustrates this more than David. His life reflects the cultural turmoil of his time. King Saul had disobeyed God's commands to the point that we read, *"...but Samuel grieved over Saul. And the Lord was sorry that he had made Saul king over Israel."* (1 Samuel 15:35) Saul's failure to carry out the Lord's commands caused Samuel the prophet of the Lord, to grieve deeply. His grief was hindering him from carrying out his leadership responsibilities as a prophet and God had to confront him. *"The Lord said to Samuel, 'How long will you grieve over Saul? I have rejected him from being king over Israel. Fill your horn with oil and set out; I will send you to Jesse the Bethlehemite, for I have provided for myself a king among his sons.'"* (1 Samuel 16:1)

The climate was ripe for conflict and crisis as it always is when leadership changes are made without an orderly system for the transferring of power and authority. Even when there is an established order for change, there is often a struggle for power among those who have been removed. The newly appointed leader must act in a way that assures his or her followers he/she will provide the needed direction. In exercising this leadership he/she will have to confront the existing power struggle that is carried over from the last administration.

When Samuel was directed to find that person who would be God's leader, he was a one man search committee that was to discern the will of the Lord in this very critical choice. After interviewing seven of Jesse's sons, he inquired if there were any other sons and Jesse responded, "There remains the youngest but he is keeping the sheep." Upon seeing him, Samuel acted immediately to anoint him and *"...the Spirit of the Lord came mightily upon David from that day forward."* (1 Samuel 16:13)

From then on, the story reveals how David worked part-time with his father's sheep and also played music for the troubled spirit of King Saul. It wasn't long until David volunteered to go to battle with Goliath, and after that victory, his reputation as a warrior soon spread among the people. His rise in popularity created tension between Saul and David, and the fact that Saul's son Jonathan was David's best friend only heightened the tension and laid the ground work for future grief.

When Saul revealed to his son Jonathan and the servants his plan to kill David, it created a dilemma for Jonathan. He would eventually have to choose between the love he had for his best friend, and the loyalty he had to his father the King. He does his best to provide David with a warning about his father's plans, and to give him time to find a safe place. Although David buys some time and is able to safely avoid being killed by Saul, he is not able to avoid the grief he experiences when he learns that both King Saul and his son Jonathan have been killed in a battle. Upon hearing the news, *"...David took hold of his clothes and tore them; and all the men who were with him did the same. They mourned and wept..."* (2 Samuel 1:11-12)

David had a sense of loyalty to the king God had anointed even though that king had plotted to kill him. Because of that loyalty, he grieved the loss of God's anointed, and his grief was compounded because of his bond with Jonathan, the king's son who was also killed. We read that David's emotional response was very public and gave permission for other men to also weep and grieve, but this is not the only way David did his grief work. David also wrote poetry as a way of getting his emotions out, and this provided a way for others to participate and share their grief, too.

2 Samuel 1:19-27 is David's poem that paints the scene of the death of Saul and Jonathan and provides directions on how Israel must respond and grieve their loss.

Personal Reflection
Read David's poem in 2 Samuel 1:19-27

David's musical ability which comforted the evil spirit of King Saul, was also used to quiet his own soul and to provide Israel a common way to express their sorrow. The songs he wrote became the hymn book for their worship. The Psalms are Israel's country music in that they contain the range of emotions from the mountain tops of joy to the darkest valley of the shadow of death. David wrote his poetry as an expression of a personal life situation that he shared as part of his own personal way of dealing with his grief and sorrow, knowing that his human emotion and need to trust God at such a time was also shared by others who lived in community with him.

This is what we hear in many of today's country music songs. Alan Jackson, in an effort to express his own personal sadness and sorrow after the terrorist attacks on 9/11, expressed his feelings in the song "Where were you when the world stopped turning, on that September Day?", He captures in his song the images of what Americans were feeling and provided us with a way to share together our common loss.

Personal Reflection
Can you think of other popular songs that express grief, sorrow, and mourning?

David follows this same pattern (2 Samuel 1:19-27) after the death of Israel's King and the King's son. For

David there was a personal degree a grief and sorrow not experienced by others in the community, but there was the common loss of leadership which they all had to face together.

Even before Saul and Jonathan's deaths David was expressing his grief over the fear of losing his life while he was on the run from Saul's army and the attempts they were making on his life. Psalm 59:1-5 was written, as the note at the beginning of the Psalm states, *"When Saul ordered his house to be watched in order to kill him."* Psalm 63 was written when he was on the run in the wilderness of Judah. David found it helpful to express his emotions in poetic words that confessed his fears and affirmed his confidence in God.

When David was imprisoned by the Philistines at Gath he wrote Psalm 56. In this letter from prison David expressed his fears that they would take his life and he had good reason to be afraid. Gath is where Goliath had lived and David obviously had a price on his head for having killed him. It is in this song from prison that he wrote those beautiful words,

"You have kept count of my toss-ings; put my tears in your bottle." (Psalm 56:8)

David was counting on God keeping track of his emotional sorrow and noticing what he was having to go through. He was expressing in song his confidence and trust that God would not fail him.

"In God, whose word I praise, in the Lord, whose word I praise, in God I trust: I am not afraid. What can a mere mortal do to me?" Psalm 56:10-11

Today we still see the importance of poetry being the expression of our grief. Many persons write their feel-ings down and read them at a funeral or memorial service to pay tribute to the deceased. When a funeral card is used that lists the information about the deceased there is usually a place on the card for a selection of poetry. The family chooses some-thing that is appropriate to celebrate the life of their loved one as well as a way of expressing spiritual truths that provide comfort and hope. Today there is also the choice of music to accompany a video presentation, and the music chosen will often have words that the family finds comforting in helping them process their loss.

David's grief experiences over the loss of his King and his beloved friend Jonathan were part of the larger community experience of grief, but he also had to cope with grief because of the death of his own children.

The David and Bathsheba story is well known and has been used for the story line of many books and movies. A very personal part of the story is often overlooked. David was told that the child, a son, who was conceived from their relationship, was to die because God was displeased with what David had done. (See 2 Samuel 11:27- 2 Samuel 12)

We are able to see in this David's experience how he grieved as he accepted the punishment for his sin, but still continued to trust that God might be gracious. When the child became ill, he expressed his sorrow and his hope by fasting day and night and he could not be convinced by those around him, that he should stop. Because he would not listen to those around him they feared telling him when the child died not knowing how he would react. To their surprise when they told him, *"He rose from the ground, washed, anointed himself, and changed his clothes. He went into the house of the Lord, and worshipped; he then went to his own house; and when he asked they set food before him and he ate."* (2 Samuel 12:20)

This kind of grieving was not under-stood by the servants and when they inquired as to why he was acting the way he was, he responded, *"While the child was still alive, I fasted and wept; for I said, 'Who knows? The Lord may be gracious to me, and the child may live.' But now he is dead why should I fast? Can I bring him back again?"* (2 Samuel 12:22-23)

In this experience of David's, we are able to glimpse what anticipatory grief may look like for the person of faith. David believes that God might be gracious and might provide the miracle of sparing the child's life, and so he prays and performs all the appropriate religious rites in hopes that the child might live. In this process he is aware of the real possibility that the child might die, so he is living between the tension of accepting the possibility of death and hoping for God to intervene. When the child dies his emotions have been spent hoping for that which did not happen. Now he must accept what his mind knew was a very real possibility. Since the child died, he realized that he had to move on knowing he was not able to change what had happened.

Because he changed so quickly, those who watched him were confused by his response. This often happens to persons when they have had time to anticipate the death of a loved one. They spend many restless nights weeping and grieving over the decline of their loved one's health. They see the physical signs of the progress of the disease and know it is "only a matter of time." But during that time, they are grieving and letting go so that when the person dies, they are able to accept it without any outburst of emotion over the death because they have spent time letting go prior to the death. People who watch the person may wonder why there are no tears at the time of death. Their observation does not have the total insight into the many restless teary nights when they worked through their grief. Observers may be surprised that a person can go back to work so quickly, or resume responsibilities that are the normal life duties. For the grieving person, the death becomes a release of what was expected, and permission to move on with their life.

That's what happened to David when his son died.

Personal Reflection
Can you identify with David's experience?

When his second son, Amnon, died it was a different kind of grief experience, because the circumstances were also very different. No two grief experiences are ever the same for anyone even though the relationships involved appear to be the same. The circumstances of Amnon's death are complicated by relationships which existed between Amnon and his brother Absalom, their sister Tamar, and their cousin Jonadab.

Amnon's rape of Tamar causes shame for David's family and after two years Absalom plans a way to kill Amnon. When he carries out his plan, his father David is told that all of his sons have been killed and David immediately begins his mourning process. Soon the process is interrupted by a report that not all of them have died, only Amnon. This is verified by the other sons upon their return home, and David hears the report of Absalom's revenge, and continues his grief for Amnon. Absalom does not return but goes into hiding. David's grief is compounded because the death of Amnon was caused by his own brother, and now David has lost them both. After three years in exile, David consented to Joab's pleading that Absalom could return to Jerusalem, but would have to stay in his own house and his father would not see him. Then, after two years, Absalom complained that he might as well have stayed where he was since he could not see his father, so Joab again was the one who convinced David to see his son. David had lived with his loss for five years and held firm to his resolve regarding Absalom, but then Absalom is permitted to see his father. He showed proper remorse and David kissed his son in an act of acceptance.

What seemed like a triumph for reconciling a father and son was only a charade. Absalom had other plans for himself; he desired to be the king and he created a conspiracy to attract the loyalty of the people of Israel. When all was said and done Absalom's warriors were defeated by David's men and it appeared that Absalom would live to fight another day. Then news came to David that

Absalom his son had been killed, and David *"...was deeply moved, and went up to the chamber over the gate, and wept; and as he went, he said, 'O my son Absalom, my son, my son Absalom! Would I had died instead of you. O Absalom, my son, my son... so the victory that day was turned into mourning for all the troops; for the troops heard that day, 'The king is grieving for his son.'"* (2 Samuel 18:33 7 19:1-2)

This experience of David grieving over the death of his son created some conflict among the troops who had risked their lives in battle to win the victory for David, because he was not celebrating the victory, but grieving his own personal loss. David was encouraged to put his grief aside for the good of the troops and go out to them and show them some praise. David's experience illustrates the difficulty for those in leadership positions to always be able to grieve appropriately when there is some conflicting issue among their followers. The expectations of leadership, by some, include a leader being able to postpone the personal expression of grief for the good of others who need comfort at that moment.

I have seen this done by pastors who had a death in their own family and they felt the need to exercise their leadership to be the source of comfort for the congregation instead of allowing themselves to express their own personal grieving emotions. I remember sitting with my mother and father and talking about their end-of-life arrangements. After buying the cemetery lots and filling out the instructions for the funeral home as to their wishes, they turned to me and said, "You will do the service, won't you?" Their question reflected the thinking that since I have done many funerals throughout my ministry, I would surely do theirs as well. When I explained to them that my love for them would cause me to grieve their passing and I would not want to be hindered in expressing whatever emotions I might feel at that time, they accepted my wishes. I did offer, however, to create the wooden urns in which their ashes would be interred, and they were pleased with that.

Parents may also be quick to feel they must refuse to show their own grieving emotions in front of their children, because they want to be strong for the entire family. This is not a good way to show children what grief looks like, for they learn from this that they should be controlling of their emotions as well.

No one answer fits all situations when it comes to choosing to openly express grieving emotions or to postpone them. No two persons ever grieve the same, and no two circumstances that create the experiences of grief are ever exactly the same. For even the same person, as we have seen with David, there are different grief responses for different losses. David's grief over Absalom was very different from that of his grief for Amnon' because the circumstances were very different. These differences not only shape the expression of grief at the time of death, but also the length of time a person will grieve.

These are not the only grief experiences of David. His life had many more times of sorrow and sadness and you only need to read the book of Psalms to see how those life events were processed through his songs.

Personal Reflection
In comparing two or more of your previous grief experiences can you identify what was similar and what was different?

Afterword

You have been reading stories of persons who have known the experience of grief. The most important story has not been any of those you have read that are written in this book. The story that matters is your own story of grief and your reflections about it as you have read each chapter. The stories you have read have been intended to trigger memories of your personal grief stories and encourage you to reflect on them and learn from them.

When someone tells us their personal story, our mind quickly sorts through our memory bank and discovers a story of equal importance which we are eager to share. It has been my hope and prayer in writing this book that the reader who reflects on their own personal story will gain a measure of strength, assurance, and comfort in remembering the support that God always provides.

It has also been my hope and prayer that these stories will enable groups of people to read them together and share their personal stories that come to mind. The settings for these shared experiences may be varied in the life of any congregation. I encourage you, now that you have read the book, to initiate a discussion among others in your congregation, whether it is in a small group ministry, bereavement support groups, care-team training, or a Sunday school class. I firmly believe that we all grow in our faith journey when we share it with others and learn from one another. During such times of sharing there may even be a few tears shed, and if that happens, be sure to affirm the promise that God will be collecting those tears also.

End Notes

Preface
1. New Living Translation Holy Bible, C 1996, 2004, by Tyndale Publishing House.
2. Richard Winter, *"A Biblical and Theological View of Grief and Bereavement,"* The Journal of Psychology and Christianity 18 (1999), p. 367)

Introduction
1. See web site Wikipedia, *"Pandora's Box",* web address: Wikipedia.org/wike/Pandora's Box
2. See Encyclopedia Mythica, *"Folk-tales: Pandora's Box"* at the following web site: pantheon.org/areas/folklore/folktales/articles/Pandora.html

3. See web site Wikipedia," *Humpty Dumpty*," Wikipedia.org/wike/ Humpty Dumpty

4. Byock, Ira M.D. *Dying Well: The Prospect for Growth at the End of Life* (New York: Riverhead Books, 1997) p.238.

5. Griffith, William H. *More Than a Partying Prayer: Lessons in Care giving for the Dying,* (Valley Forge, PA: Judson Press, 2004) p.68

6. Prend, Ashley Davis, *Transcending Loss, Understanding the Lifelong Impact on Grief and How to Make it Meaningful,* New York, Berkley Books, p. xix

Chapter 1

1. Millspaugh, Dick, "Assessment and Response to Spiritual Pain: Part I", Journal of Palliative Medicine, Volume 8, Number 5, 2005 p.920)

2. Lynette J. Hoy, NCC, LCPC, "The Only Way Out of Grief is Through" Frequently Asked Questions, web site: counselcareconnection.org/

articles/79/3Understanding Grief/Page3.html

Chapter 3

1. See Hospice Net: *Journaling*, web site: hospicent.org/html/read26. html
2. Bob Deits, *Life after Loss*, (Cambridge, MA, Lifelong Books 2004) p.204
3. "David's mother's name (Nitzevet) does not appear in the Torah, but rather is recorded in the Talmud, Tractate Bava Batra 91a." See web site, *Ask the Rabbi*, ohr.edu/ask/ ask221.htm#Q4 "David's Mother"

Chapter 7

1. McGlauflin, Helene, Med. LCPC, "*Dominoes: A Metaphor for Helping Grieving Children, Teens, and their Families,*" Healing Ministry, Volume 9, Number 2, March/April 2002, p.53